I CAN'T SEE YOU, I'M DEAF

A Memoir

Woody Livingston

Olive Juice Publishing

Rochester, New York

Woody Livingston/Olive Juice Publishing
Rochester, New York

Editor: Joshua Stuart

Book Layout © 2019 BookDesignTemplates.com

I Can't See You, I'm Deaf/ Woody Livingston. -- 1st ed.
ISBN 978-1-7331618-0-0

CONTENTS

CHAPTER ONE

THE RADIO

I was five-years-old and walking through the corridor of a strange building with my parents. I was disoriented and had no idea why I was there. The floor of the hallway was checkered with big black and white tiles. As we walked, I made giant steps trying my hardest to only land on the black ones, pretending the white ones were puddles of water. I always enjoyed jumping over puddles on rainy days, feeling the "clumping" vibration made by my shoes with every hop.

When we came to a stop, I noticed there were chairs along one wall. We walked over to a desk with a woman sitting behind it. There was a black telephone with a long cord on her desk and I wanted nothing more than to pick it up and say "Hello!" Next to the phone was a typewriter. Stacks of paper were scattered everywhere.

I watched intently as my dad spoke to the woman but didn't understand what he was saying. When he was finished speaking with her, we went back and sat down in the corridor chairs.

Once seated, I simply looked down at my brown Hush-Puppies shoes. I was so bored and swung my legs back and forth as I watched strange people walk back and forth through the hallway. I stared at their feet to see if they were walking on the black or white tiles—imagining that anyone who would step on the white tiles would get wet. Each time they did I would say, "splash!"

One person who walked past looked like a doctor. He was carrying a clipboard and wearing a white long shirt. He glanced down at me and smiled. *Am I at a hospital?* I thought. *Is there something wrong with me?* I had no idea. I continued swinging my legs as if I was walking above the floor. My mother shot me a look and put her hands on my legs to stop me from swinging.

A tall, thin man approached and began talking with my mother and father. I still could not understand what was being said and I really didn't care. "My name is Bob, how are you?" the man in white said to me and smiled. "Are you ready?" he asked, extending his hand. He was nice but he spoke to me in a very slow voice, almost like I was stupid. But most adults treated me like this; maybe it was because I could never hear a thing they were saying. I didn't like people talking to me like I was stupid or different.

I got up, waved goodbye to my parents, and walked with Bob to a weird room with tiny holes in the walls, except for a small window. Next to the window was a set of headphones and some toys on the table. Bob then pointed to a chair in the middle of the room, which faced the window and told me to sit down. Then he shut the door that looked a lot like a refrigerator door and sat down with me. I wanted to play with the toys, but I was drawn to the box Bob was opening. *Am I getting a gift?* I wondered. *Is today my birthday?*

Bob was taking something out of the box that looked like a radio. I watched intently as he installed the batteries. I was super interested and asked what the thing was.

"It's a hearing aid," he said with a warm smile.

I was still clueless. *A hearing aid? Is that like lemonade? Why do none of these adults make any sense?* I was beginning to like Bob because he was nice and friendly to me and I had an easier time figuring out what was he saying because he gestured with his hands a lot. He then pulled a strap out of the package. He began putting it over my shirt and snapped the strap together over my chest. I noticed it had a pocket right in the middle of my chest. Bob then inserted the "hearing aid" into the pocket and ran a long cord from the device into an earpiece. He then took the earpiece and gently snapped it into my ear. At first, I was afraid that it was going to hurt and was relieved when it didn't.

I watched him put his fingers on the hearing aid again to turn it on, at which point he asked, "Can you hear me?" I didn't understand him, and I didn't respond. He turned the volume control higher and I could actually hear his fingers rubbing on the microphone. It sounded like a paper bag being crushed. He took his fingers off the dial and asked me again, "Can you hear me?"

I was awestruck. "Wow!" I exclaimed. "Yes, I can hear you!" As he moved around, I began to hear so many loud noises. He pointed to the window in the room and explained that he was going into the next room and wanted me to look at the window. Then he got up and opened the push handle on the funny looking door. He closed it and I heard a popping noise similar to the sound of closing a refrigerator. *Cool.* I thought. Within seconds, Bob appeared in the other room and I could see him through the window. He was waving at me to get my attention. I was wondering what he was going to do. I could see that in front of him there was a device with controls and a big microphone.

"Can you hear me?" he asked.

"Yes." I nodded.

"I'm going to say a few words and you repeat after me, okay?"

I nodded my head once again. Bob got close to the microphone and began saying words like "baseball," "cowboy," and many others. When he was done, Bob didn't bother to take the hearing aid off of me. He casually opened the door and walked me to my parents.

Alongside Bob, I became startled by the noises I could now hear in the hallway. My eyes darted back and forth at everyone's shoes because I could hear them making loud tapping noises on the floor. I could even hear someone close a door further down the hall. Fear and confusion turned into amusement at the loud sounds and the fact that I could recognise what they were.

While Bob began talking to my parents, I started wandering around the hallway listening to the loud voices of people in conversation. I heard the secretary at the desk typing on her big typewriter. She smiled at me and I smiled back.

"Here, let me help you with your jacket," my mother called out while practically chasing me down the hallway. I was thrilled by all the new noises and sounds and echoes while walking down the stairs and out of the building. I was happy I could hear the incredible sounds all around me but sadly my hearing aid didn't change the fact that most people talked down to me or treated me like I was stupid—the hearing aid only made it worse. Even at five I knew I hated this, and from then on it was me against the world.

CHAPTER TWO

MRS. EVILLA

I couldn't wait to go back to school with my new "radio." It was my first day in the first-grade. When I got to school I walked right into my new classroom and put away my lunch box in the cloakroom. I could smell the food inside it and knew I was going to have a peanut butter and jelly sandwich for lunch; my favorite.

The students sat at small wooden desks, and I chose one right by the big windows. I lifted the top lid and admired all the crayons and pencils inside the desk. I've always loved the smell of wooden pencils and coloring with crayons. *This is going to be fun*, I told myself. I turned up the volume on my hearing aid and immediately noticed that the classroom was very noisy with the sound of the children's conversations, but I didn't understand what they were saying. I sat and looked around with wonder. I noticed the ABC prints above the blackboard. Looking at the big and small print of each letter I thought, *can I really learn to write like that?*

But my dreams for the future instantly popped like balloons at the end of a birthday party. Mrs. Evilla, our teacher, started class by yelling at the entire classroom. I didn't understand a thing that she was yelling. I checked the volume on my hearing aid, which was all the way up. Maybe there were too many other noises in the classroom, but I didn't think so. All I remember about her was that she looked really old, with thick, grey hair, and a stern looking face. Once she stopped yelling the first thing she did was place a big stick on her desk for everyone to see. I was instantly terrified of Mrs. Evilla.

As the day went on I noticed that there was a pencil sharpener on the wall by the blackboard, very close to my desk. I knew I had many un-sharpened pencils and so I became interested in playing with the pencil sharpener. I got up from my desk so Mrs. Evilla could see me. "Can I sharpen my pencils?" I asked sheepishly, hoping my question wouldn't make her want to swing her big stick at me.

"Go ahead," she snarled.

I practically skipped with glee over to the pencil sharpener and in-serted them one after the other and had such fun! I sharpened all my pencils but one, and with the last pencil I decided to see just how far it could go. I was having fun with my experiment when Mrs. Evilla took notice and yelled at me, "What are you doing?"

I quickly backed away, leaving my last pencil in the sharpener. Mrs. Evilla took out short nub of a pencil and pressed it close to my face. She looked at me angrily and yelled, "Get back to your seat!"

I jumped back toward my seat and sat back down. *Why is she so upset about my pencils?* I thought.

As the year went on my time with Mrs. Evilla could only be de-scribed as a nightmare. Whenever the class misbehaved, Mrs. Evilla would tell us, "There is a man watching over you from the door." The classroom doors had big windows in them that would frighten me. I was pretty sure that whenever I turned to look through them a man with a big beard would be peering through the glass. I was afraid of him too; afraid that he was going to take one of us away to a place to be beaten or something worse. I was confused and felt lost.

I had a hard time understanding Mrs. Evilla and I wondered if I was hearing as well as the other students. The nightmare continued every day until one day it got even worse. I was sitting at my desk and, Greg, who sat at the desk next to mine, came in to class late. When he took his seat, I couldn't help but notice that he had a bandage wrapped all around his nose. I could tell by his expressions that he was in pain and was convinced the bearded man from the hallway had beaten him. It made me so afraid I couldn't even ask him about it. In fact, I was so scared I couldn't even bring myself to ask Mrs. Evilla if I could go to the bathroom. *What if the man beyond the doors of the classroom would come after me?* Nope, I was going to stay in my seat! No matter how badly I had to go, I was not moving.

Eventually and embarrassingly so, I ended up soiling my pants. Mrs. Evilla, who took notice and was thoroughly disgusted, decided to call my mom to come take me home. I had no idea if I was hearing properly or if I misunderstood what was going on in class, but surely, I was very uncomfortable in that first-grade classroom.

CHAPTER THREE

THE MAINSTREAM 1966

Because of increased early detection of hearing loss and advances in hearing technology, more and more deaf and hard of hearing children are learning in their neighborhood schools, instead of specialized programs. Mainstreaming is a term used to describe the integration of children with hearing loss into regular school classrooms so they can learn alongside their hearing peers. This now happens at earlier ages than ever before, with so many children mainstreaming as early as preschool.
~The Clark School

My mom sat us down one day at the dining table and made an announcement to me and my two hearing-impaired sisters. "You'll be going to a mainstream school," she said and explained that we would also be in classes with other hearing-impaired students which would help us understand and communicate better in other hearing classes. My oldest sister would be in the same school with me, and my younger sister would go to a different school.

I was excited and relieved about not having to go back to the old school again with Mrs. Evilla. I wondered if I was going to the mainstream school because I couldn't understand Mrs. Evilla. But I didn't care because I was happy to be going to a new school and getting away from her.

On my first day at the new school, I walked into my classroom with my Beatles metal lunch box. It was a classroom for the hearing impaired. I stood at the doorway with my sister, Patty, not knowing what to expect. The teacher approached me and kindly introduced herself.

"Hi, I'm Mrs. Wise." The white name tag on her blue blouse confirmed she was telling the truth.

Then we were introduced to the five other students sitting at their desks. Each desk had a nametag in front of it written in black marker on a colored paper. I could actually smell the fresh magic marker. I spotted my name tag sitting on a desk a few feet away. The name tag was blue, my favorite color. I was happy and eager to learn. The friendly teacher, Mrs. Wise, had everything prepared. The classroom was well organized, with colorful posters and calendars. There was a round table in the corner of the room with bookshelves on both side of the walls and the floor was half-carpeted. There were even kids who had the same body hearing aids as I did. They quickly became my "radio" friends. Some kids had smaller ear hearing aids that hooked over the ears. I had to wear the body hearing aid like some others because I needed more powerful technology.

It was a small classroom and we would sit in one row facing the blackboard. Mrs. Wise made sure each one of us understood everything she was saying. It was comfortable and I felt connected and safe. I could finally understand what was being said. She knew how to communicate with us, if we had any questions or had to go to the bathroom all we had to do was raise our hands. I was so relieved.

Mrs. Wise explained that the class room was equipped with a loop system that would connect to our hearing aids once we turned on the switch on our hearing aids to "T" (telephone) mode. Mrs. Wise would talk into her microphone that was clipped to her blouse. We would hear her speak much louder with less background interference. I liked it because it reminded me of being in the soundproof room when Bob spoke to me through a microphone.

I had second grade math in the hearing classes. Math was easy for me to figure out and the teacher was easy to understand, because I sat in the front row. She would talk in front of me making sure I was lipreading and listening to her. I enjoyed her math classes.

There were times when walking in the hallway from my hearing classes to my homeroom class that I had to endure stares and badgering questions. Kids were amused by the large hearing aid on my chest. They had no idea what it was and looked at me like I was an alien from outer space. "What is that thing in your ear?" some kids would ask or "Is that a radio?"

No matter how many times they asked, the teachers would have to tell them, "it is not polite to ask."

At first it didn't bother me when kids were curious about my hearing aid because I thought they wanted to learn about me. But soon I grew tired of the same questions and attention. A few times, I pretended I was listening to music, bouncing my head around in front of a group of kids at the table in the lunch room. They looked at me with jealousy as if they wanted to listen along with me. The kids thought I was going to get in trouble for having a "radio" in school. Having a sense of humor helped me cope with the other students.

I remembered once talking to a deaf girl in class. She had a hard time understanding speech and lipreading was difficult for her. I tried using my hands to communicate with her, but the teacher slapped my hands away and told me not to use gestures or signs with my hands. "Why can't I use my hands to make her understand me?" I asked Mrs. Wise.

"Because your speech and lipreading skills would get worse," she answered. "Now, get back to your desk; break is over."

I never understood why I couldn't sign, but my speech did improve.

Mrs. Wise noticed I was memorizing all the spelling words, but not understanding the pronunciation of the words. I was always great in spelling but I couldn't make the proper sounds when I tried to say them aloud. Mrs. Wise called me over to her desk. I watched her opening up the dictionary and I looked at her like in disgust because I hated dictionaries. Mrs. Wise tried to show me how words are pronounced in the dictionary. I really wanted to learn from a person teaching me how to pronounce a word orally rather than try to learn from the dictionary because it was hard for me to read the symbols in the dictionary. I began to realize if I wanted to speak well, I had to learn to pronounce words correctly. I worked harder at speaking, lipreading, and paying attention in class to succeed in the hearing classes.

Mainstream art classes were one of my favorite subjects along with math and physical education. I watched my classmate Robert do pastel drawings and I was amazed by his work. He was a burgeoning artist and definitely had a gift. I wanted to draw like he did and the challenge made me realize that I had some artistic skills also. I was greatly influenced by the art classes.

After fifth grade, I was ready to go to a mainstream school. I had no idea what it would be like or if the kids and teachers in my new school would treat me different because of my hearing aid. But I wouldn't let them; I was going to be brave and prove to everyone that I was the same as they were with or without a "radio" strapped to my chest.

CHAPTER FOUR

WILD, WILD BRUCE

I walked into the two-story brick building called the Bruce School in Lawrence, Massachusetts. It was an old school and well built. I was finally going to an all-hearing school with friends who grew up with me from my neighborhood. My most vivid memory was entering the front of the building, which faced Butler Street, and jogging up the stairs to find my 6th grade classroom on the second floor. I walked into the classroom and saw a blondish teacher, probably in her mid-thirties standing by her desk. She smiled and noticed I was wearing a hearing aid.

"You must be Woody," she said, adjusting her glasses on the bridge of her nose.

"Yes."

"I'm Mrs. Peacock." Her initial smile showed she was friendly. But she also looked tough and strict and somebody not to be messed with. I decided I had to be cautious around her.

The classroom was big with windows from one end to the other. Mrs. Peacock showed me to my graffiti laden desk. I was used to being comfortable and safe in a disciplined mainstreamed school. Something about the graffiti told me I was about to face a wild bunch of students. I sensed trouble right away when I got dirty looks from some of the guys. I gave it right back at them. I wanted to be in the hearing world and I knew I would have to persevere to stay in it. I was not afraid at all. I was fearless and knew I was going to face some obstacles.

Sixth grade at the Bruce School wasn't as hard as I thought it would be, but I hated English and Social Studies because most of the lessons were verbal and I couldn't understand what the teacher were saying unless she sat with me in a one-to-one discussion.

It took little time for kids to start harassing me for wearing a large hearing aid, but it made me more resilient. I started to stand up for myself. I learned to avoid fighting unless I had to defend myself. I had my limits. When kids wanted to pick a fight with me the hard part was walking away from it.

Whenever I finished my assignment or project in class, I would draw pictures of people and objects. One student loved my drawings. He had an interest in drawing with me. He was a big kid and we quickly became friends, which gave me confidence. I once drew a picture of Mrs. Peacock being tough with her hair looking like a peacock.

"What are you drawing Woody?" Mrs. Peacock asked as she walked up to my desk. "Can I see your drawings?"

She did ask nicely so I handed them over. She looked at them as if she was enjoying my artwork. She then burst out laughing while the class looked on and I thought I was going to get in trouble. Nobody ever made her laughed like that.

"You're creative," she said. "I like it!"

"Well…thanks?" I wasn't trying to be mean with my drawing, but was I really going to get away with this?

She laughed again. If you ever saw her with a mean expression on her face when she got upset, you made sure to get out of her way!

There was always excitement in the classroom and I was amazed how tough Mrs. Peacock was when she handled the students. I think she was from the Bronx. One time, two students were arguing, and when two more joined a little brawl broke out. Everybody was pushing and shoving each other. I watched Mrs. Peacock grab a kid and throw him out of the way and then grab another and forced him into his seat. She yelled at the kids like she was from the military.

Another time she got fed up with sending a tall kid named John to the principal, so she moved his desk into a closet and told him to stay here. It was wild because John wouldn't shut his mouth, so Mrs.

Peacock slammed the closet door on him until he stopped talking. Some of the students were scared of her. She was energetic, and after a while nobody dared to cross Mrs. Peacock.

But she was always friendly to me and I liked her for that. Maybe she thought I wasn't part of the zoo.

The Substitute Teacher

Since I could not hear high–pitched sounds well, I would turn up my hearing aid to hear Mrs. Peacock a little better, and my earpiece would emit a high-pitched whistle. It was embarrassing. Mrs. Peacock would repeatedly call me out, "Woody, can you fix that noise, please?" I would have to turn down the volume to stop the noise which reduced my understanding of her speaking.

One time, a substitute teacher, Mrs. White, had to replace Mrs. Peacock, who was out sick. I decided to play a trick on Mrs. White who was young and new at her job. When she was writing on the blackboard, I loosened my ear mold and made it squeal and Mrs. White reacted oddly. With her blue eyes blazing, she looked around the classroom and then up at the ceiling as if a UFO were landing on the roof. "What is that noise?" she asked the class.

No one said anything so she continued to write on the board. I made the earpiece squeal again. This time, she opened the classroom door and looked out in the hallway. Everyone in class started laughing.

Mrs. White stormed back in, "All right, who's doing this?"

A girl stood up and told on me, "It's coming from Woody's hearing aid. He doesn't always know when it's making the noise."

Mrs. White looked at me and said, "I don't want to hear that noise again." Then she laughed knowing she had been tricked.

The Rock

Recess was held in a big school yard. We played rubber ball or dodgeball or would just hang out. One beautiful day, I was standing in the schoolyard talking to a friend. Everyone was running around making a lot of noises. This weird girl behind me threw a big rock the size of a brick in the air and yelled to watch out causing everyone to scatter. I had no idea what was going on and the rock landed dead center on my head. I felt as if I had been struck by lightning. Blood was dripping all over my face and shirt, but I didn't pass out. My friends were scared, and a good friend grabbed me and ran us to the nurse. I sprinted across the big play yard, through the school's door, and down the hallway dripping a trail of blood. It was a marathon to the nurse. My pristine white shirt was almost completely red. Right away the nurse put ice on my head and I was taken to the hospital for few stitches.

The next day, Mrs. Peacock gave me a big hug and sat me down with a group of girls. "It was a girl who threw a rock at me!" I said to Mrs. Peacock.

"You'll be fine with *them*," she giggled.

I admired that woman, even though there were some things that weren't right about her—she was a fighter. She stood up for herself and didn't take any rubbish from anyone. A good role model for me.

Bruce School was like a war zone for me; it was wild, but it made me stronger and wiser. It gave me courage and was the beginning of my independence, teaching me how stand up for myself, and learning how to deal with the hearing world in the face of insults and brick-sized rocks to the head, just as Mrs. Peacock dealt with her classroom.

CHAPTER FIVE

THE RADIO'S LAST DAYS

Boys Club of America was one of my favorite places to play sports or hang out with friends. There was swimming, boxing, weight lifting, basketball, floor hockey, pool, and many other activities. I moved on from wearing a strap that carried around my *radio* for several years and played sports with it tucked away in a pocket. As a teenager it was a real pain in the butt. I would always be listening to the sound at waist level instead at chest level, where the microphone was. I played through with it a lot during floor hockey games in the Boys Club's damp, old gym. Every once in a while, the annoying hearing aid would pop out of my pocket, go flying across the gym floor, and I would have to yell at the referee for a quick time out. He would blow the whistle, everybody had to stop playing, and I would yell, "don't move," so nobody would step on the lost hearing aid. The referee would find it and hand it back to me while everybody watched me put it back on. I was always relieved it still worked.

"Okay, I can hear now," I would say. "Let's play!"

I refused to wear the strap that held the hearing aid as a teenager. I hated it. The white strap looked just like a bra for women, except it had a pocket in the middle of my chest for the hearing aid. I had to change in the locker room at the Boys Club and there was no way I would wear the Radio strap and have all the boys thinking I'm wearing a bra.

My Radio Drowned

When I was nine-years-old, my parents took me to a boy's camp called the LaSalle. The camp was fun, with many sports and indoor and outdoor activities. I spent much of my time fishing and rowing boats, and even won a rowing contest.

One day, I went to the end of the dock and started fishing. There was nobody around, just me with my fishing rod. There was a tug on my fishing line and suddenly I lost my balance and fell into the water. That would have been okay, but my foot got caught in the dock. I frantically fought to stay afloat, but I kept sinking, swinging my arms and making splashing noises. I was gasping for air, bobbing in and out of the water. I thought I was going to drown. Finally, a camp instructor ran over and pulled me up out of the water and loosened my foot caught between the dock boards. I was scared and shaken up, and suddenly I couldn't hear anything. I had killed the *radio!* My hearing aid!

I was glad the camp instructor was around to save me. My life was more important than the hearing aid that I hated so much. The camp counsellor called my mom. "I've got bad news for you," he said. "Woody's hearing aid fell in the water, but Woody's okay." I don't think he told my mother that I had a near drowning.

For the rest of camp, I had to concentrate hard to read lips. The instructors went out of their way to make it easier for me to read lips. I wasn't used to being totally deaf, but luckily, I had a few adults to help me out and used gestures to communicate about what was going on during camp.

At the camp, I was more comfortable with people I could communicate with than with the people that that I couldn't understand. I hung out with the ones I felt were easy to communicate with and avoided the ones I couldn't understand. I hated being isolated or left out. Losing my *radio* taught me that I could survive without a hearing aid and winning a camp trophy for "best athlete" was a big boost to my confidence.

The Radio Thief

I remember having to deal with a tough situation over my radio. It was a breezy and spring-like day. I had stepped out of the Boy's Club and crossed a street and reached the sidewalk. It was the same route I took to get home every day. I could hear the wind on my radio, which was clipped in my shirt pocket. Up ahead I saw a boy coming down from a hill to the sidewalk. I froze briefly and realized that I had seen him around before. I knew he liked to beat up kids and he was trouble.

Minding my own business, I looked down on the sidewalk hoping he wouldn't bother me, but he blocked my way and pushed me around. I thought *here we go again*. Yes, again, because I had been bullied many times. I didn't want to face another guy like him.

The kid, who was bigger than me, demanded, "Give me your radio!"

Feeling trapped I protested. "It's not a radio, it's a hearing aid!"

"You're lying," he grunted. "It looks like a radio. Let me listen!"

"Sure," I said. I gave him the ear piece and a whiny, high-pitch whistle screamed out from it.

He was a little startled by it, but I was powerless to say more. I was hoping there wouldn't be a fight and I didn't want to get hurt. I was nervous. He put the ear-piece to his ear like he was unsure about what to do with it and listened. That moment was priceless. His face lit up in shock and pain and that even scared me more. He reacted as if someone had screamed into his ear and I was pretty sure he screamed too, but I didn't hear it because he had my ear piece. He jerked it out of his ear and angrily threw it at me and then shoved me out of the way. By the time I put my ear piece back on he was gone.

I was relieved that I didn't lose the hearing aid or get punched in the face over a "radio." It wasn't the first time I had to defend myself for wearing the hearing aid. People usually got it mistaken for a pocket radio, which would often get me in trouble. I always feared for the worse when someone asked me about it.

Sometimes I thought it would have been easier just being *deaf* than beaten up.

During the summer before I started high school, I was crossing Water Street on my way to the Boy's Club. There was a grocery store next to the club and I crossed the street unaware that a robbery was in progress. I walked past the grocery store and four kids who had been robbing the store ran out. One of them grabbed me and put a knife in my face because the cops were coming. He was yelling at me about something. "If you're telling me anything, I can't hear you."

The robber decided to let me go, since the cops were closing in. He yelled something at me again and ran across the field behind the Boys Club and jumped the fence near the Merrimac River as the police were chasing them on foot.

I looked toward the Boys Club, and all the boys were looking through the window. I waved to them.

When I walked into the Boys Club, some of the boys told me they had seen the kid with the knife. But I calmly participated in my activities as though nothing had happened.

Sometimes I thought about that event. *What would have happened if I'd been a hearing person? Did telling him that I was hearing impaired make the robber realize I'd be useless? Did the high-pitch noise from my hearing aid scare him off?* My hearing impairment did have its advantages every once in a while.

High School

My first day in high school started badly. I was sitting at an art desk in the back of the room with a few other students. I wore a black tie, dress pants, and dress shoes. Mrs. Hopkins, my shop teacher, was doing roll call. She had called my name, but I didn't respond. "Is Woody here?" she asked again.

One student, Sue, pointed me out. Mrs. Hopkins gave me a serious look. She yelled at me to go to the infirmary to get my hearing checked.

I told her it would be a waste of time. "Do you want detention?" she asked thinking I was giving her an attitude.

Luckily, Sue, who was my 8th grade classmate, came to my defense. "He's hearing impaired and he can only read lips."

Mrs. Hopkins gestured to me to come up front. "From now on, I want you to be at the front every morning when I do roll calls."

"Well, now you know about me," I said with a defiant smirk.

The students around me tried not to laugh, but Mrs. Hopkins gave me a warning look. That was not a good first day for a hearing–impaired student in a hearing high school.

The School Bus

Living with deafness and wearing a hearing aid in high school was fraught with perils, which I learned the hard way.

I had to take the bus to school and one day I got on the bus and looked for an empty seat. There were a few left and I sat at a vacant spot next to a pretty girl who sat by a window. The girl said something to me which I didn't understand. But I assumed it wasn't important and didn't bother asking what she had said. The bus drove on to school and dropped us off.

When my English class was dismissed, I walked out the door into the hallway and a tall student, a senior, grabbed my shirt and yelled some profanities. He punched me in the face and my glasses went flying off and then he fled. I was stunned and had no idea why I was attacked. I had assumed he didn't like me because I was deaf. I went to tell Mrs. Hopkins what happened instead of going after the idiot. When she found the student, he admitted he was angry at me because his girlfriend from the bus was saving a seat for him and he was peeved off that I took it. Apparently that morning on the bus his girlfriend tried to warn me but I didn't bother to ask her to repeat it for me.

From then on I decided that whenever I didn't understand something, I had to be brave and ask the person to repeat themselves. Not making that effort would lead to conflicts. I didn't deserve to get hurt that way and the senior was suspended. His friends didn't take the outcome well and approached me in the school's cafeteria, tipping over my food and telling me I was going to die. It wasn't a pleasant scene and I had to control myself. Fortunately, some of my football friends stood up for me and told the guys to lay off. It was a scary day and I thought I handled it well because I avoided a brawl over the miscommunication on the bus that morning.

Goodbye Radio, Goodbye!

Hearing aid technology was improving in 1975 and my parents were able to get me a new over–the–ear hearing aid. With it, I heard well— good enough to hear a whistle. It was a big relief. No more wearing that big, fat, annoying boxy hearing aid! I grew my hair a little bit long and it covered the new processor over my left ear. No one would know I had a hearing aid or could tell I was deaf. I was happy to be able to play soccer for my high school without the wires dangling out of my shirt. Ten years of wearing that radio had finally came to an end! I was so relieved; it was like I had been freed from awkward-deaf-puberty prison after ten years. I never forget the first day I wore the new hearing aid to school. I was sitting at the art desk with three other students and they noticed that I wasn't wearing the *radio* any more. I was drawing and a long-haired-girl came behind me. She was testing if I could hear. She was calling out my name softly, "Woody... Woody."

"Yes dear?" I said nonchalantly

She gasped. "How did you hear me?"

I showed off my new hearing aid hanging over my ear. She was amazed. I felt good to not have to hear that old constant "*is that a radio?*" question. Once in a while someone would let it slip and I'd tell them, "I killed it!"

CHAPTER SIX

I CAN'T?

As you can imagine, growing up in a hearing world can be tough for a hearing-impaired person. But for me it was even more challenging to be constantly confronted by so many people who kept on telling me, "No, you can't, because you're deaf."

I was stubborn and I didn't listen (no pun intended). I was determined to not let them discourage me from pursuing my dreams and aspirations. I wanted—no, *needed* to prove they were wrong.

On a day in May, a perfect day for a game of baseball, I was thirteen years old and playing left field. I WAS wearing my beloved Boston Red Sox baseball hat cap during a tryout for the Tower Hill Twins baseball club. I remembered the coach yelled out from the pitcher's mound, "Woody, you're after this batter. Go get ready!"

I didn't quite hear everything else he said, but it only took a little common sense to figure it out when he pointed and waved me over to the bench. I jogged over to where all the baseball helmets and bats were scattered around on the ground. I looked at the bats and selected the right size for me and put on the navy-blue helmet.

A kid got up from the wooden bench, walked up to me and said, "You're not going to make the team because you're deaf." He was emphatic about this but I just laughed at him.

"Just watch me," I told the kid. "Maybe you won't make the team because your mouth is too big." I walked to the plate and got ready for the coach throw a pitch to me. I was determined to prove Big Mouth wrong and told to myself, *I'm going to scare that kid with a foul ball.*

The coach pitched the ball and *whack*! I grounded the ball toward the bench, forcing Big Mouth to dive for safety. "Did that shut your mouth?" I yelled out. I heard laughter from the kids nearby, from the field, and even from the coach who couldn't stop laughing. The next pitch sailed out of the ball park. As it disappeared, I looked back at the kid, "Did you see that one? I might be deaf but I'm not blind!"

When the tryout ended, the coach gathered all of us together and made an announcement who made the team. "You made the team Woody," he said nonchalantly and threw me a uniform. This was a big moment for me. Deaf or not, I proved Big Mouth wrong and that I could do whatever I wanted. My ability to play on the diamond was a dream come true and added confidence in my ability to succeed in life.

Unfortunately, older folks could be just as bad as the kids I was growing up with. They had the mindset that a deaf person shouldn't be allowed to do anything. I met up with my friend Jeff one day to go out for a ride on our 10-speed bicycles. Jeff's father was fixing his bike and noticed that I was wearing a hearing aid. I'd never met Jeff's father before and it hurt to hear him tell me, "Deaf people shouldn't ride bicycles because they can't hear the cars." I was speechless. An adult telling me I couldn't do anything.

"Deaf people aren't stupid," I said laying into Jeff's father. "Sure, we can't hear. But we're more cautious than hearing people because we use our eyes and not our ears. You can't hear a pothole yell *watch out potholes.* You've got to look out for it."

I'll never forget the look on his face. He looked at me and smiled. "Good point! Enjoy your bike ride, boys. Keep your eyes on the road."

The fact that I stood up to adults like Jeff's dad taught me a valuable lesson I'd never forget. Someone listened to me and understood. Deaf or not I could speak up and be seen and heard.

My encounter with Jeff's dad was not forgotten later when I was browsing among some vendors in the school gym during eighth-grade.

It was a Career Day for the eighth graders and I had to figure what I wanted to do with my life. I stopped at the booth manned by my English teacher that had information on professional fields such as law and medicine. I was thoroughly interested and picked up a few brochures.

"You *can't* become a doctor or lawyer," my English teacher said. "In those professions you have to be able to hear well."

Taken aback, I looked at him and glared. "With that kind of logic, I can skip English classes too, because you think I'm too deaf and stupid to become a lawyer."

A woman standing next to me burst into a little laughter. She put her hand on my shoulder. "Don't ever let anyone stop you from doing whatever you want to do," she said with a smile.

That was the Seventies and many people did not understand deafness. They always assumed you couldn't do anything because you were hearing impaired. The more obstacles I ran into, the more it made me want to do anything I desired and aspired to. I made a rule, a personal vow to myself: *Never say, "I can't."*

Fishing

My dad was keenly interested in the outdoors, especially fishing and hunting. I enjoyed fishing trips with him when I was young. One of my favorite fishing trips was going with my father to a pond in Dracut, Massachusetts. Fishing was relaxing and it was fun to see what kind of fish you caught. I didn't like catching sunfish or kibbes because they were too small and had sharp fins and were difficult to unhook.

One day we paddled out in a small wooden boat to the middle of the pond and drifted there, watching the reeds waving in the distance. At times my dad would let me row the boat, and I loved it. My dad had put a frog lure on his line and I used a live worm on mine. We cast them into the water with the round red and white bobbers on the lines. Sure enough, after a while, my dad felt a tug. "Are you getting a bite?" I asked him softly.

My dad swung the fishing line past himself, hooking the fish and we saw the big splash.

"Do you think it's a big fish?" I asked.

"I hope so!" He said, grunting while struggling with the fish.

As he carefully reeled the fish to the side of the boat, he found that it was too heavy to reel into the boat. I watched my dad dip his arm in the water while holding his rod. He grabbed the fish's gill and pulled it out of the water. When he landed it aboard, we were stunned beyond disbelief. "Wow!" we both said at the same time.

It was a big largemouth bass, probably more than 10 lbs. It even bent the hooks on the lure. Any fisherman would be proud to land one.

We pulled a few more smaller fish in, and then as the time passed, we got wrapped up in the surroundings and simply enjoyed what was a great day. The sun was setting and a red glow washed over the reeds. The water was still. Everything was quiet, and peaceful. It was a moment that encouraged me to be more optimistic—anything extraordinary could happen, whether I could hear it or not. I closed my eyes so I could feel the rocking of the wooden boat and the warmth of the air. It was a perfect moment. Father and son. Fishing was a great reminder that not only could I do some things just as well as hearing people—I could do them better.

CHAPTER SEVEN

SEE NO BALL

I walked into the Dust Bowl ballpark of South Lawrence, Massachusetts in my Tower Hill baseball uniform. I dropped my things by the visitor's bench and grabbed my glove and joined my teammates for a pregame warm-up on the field of the old ballpark. The coach soon called us all in to gather together. He called out the players' names and the positions they would be starting, "Woody, you're playing left field."

I was delighted. Jogging to left field, I thought to myself, *I get to start the game! This is going to be wicked!*

While waiting for the game to start, I warmed up with the center fielder. The pitcher finished warming up, and the umpire yelled, "Play ball!" It was a beautiful evening, full of cheers from the crowd. There were fly balls, pop flies, grounders, and a few nail–biting moments. As the game went into the last inning, which would be the seventh inning, the sun was just beginning to set. There I was in left field with two outs, and the only thing I could think about was, *I can't wait to get up at bat!*

The batter swung! There was a pop fly coming toward me. Suddenly I couldn't see the ball. Where was it? I yelled, looking all around in a panic. Thud! The ball landed on the ground grass about three feet in front of me. Quickly, I picked up the ball and threw it to third base as the runner slid into the base.

"Safe!" as the third baseman dropped the ball. I looked back and saw the other team was laughing at me. I was so embarrassed that I couldn't see a fly ball. When the inning was over, I approached the team's bench, dreading about what the coach would say. He was standing, arms folded, waiting for me, looking ready to give me a lecture.

"What in the world happened out there?" Coach asked.

"I have no idea!"

"Make sure you get an eye test when you get home," he said. "You're up third at bat, so get ready."

As the first two players struck out and I was coming up to bat, we were losing 6–0. The Mets pitcher had a no–hitter going. He was my good friend Paul, and he was the best pitcher in the league that year with his nasty curve balls.

I got to the plate and was getting settled in, I looked directly at Paul. He looked at me. He knew I could lipread well. "I'm going to get you," he said.

I smiled. Since he had a no–hitter in the game, I was determined to get a hit, especially after making that error in left field. I figured that if I got a hit, people would forget about my embarrassing error.

As Paul was winding up, I assumed he was going to throw a curve ball. I think he had forgotten that we used to practice playing ball with each other, so I would know how he pitched. He threw a curve and I hit the ball on a line drive to center field. I pumped my fist rounding into first, breaking my good friend's Paul's no–hitter. I had the last laugh.

When the game was over and as I gathered my stuff to leave the park, my coach reminded me again. "Get an eye test."

As I walked out of the park, my grandfather was waiting for me in his blue pickup truck. "I saw the last inning of the game," he said. "How come you couldn't see the ball?"

"I don't know."

"You might need glasses," he said shrugging his shoulders.

I didn't want to think about wearing glasses, but the following week, my mom took me to the local eye doctor, who determined that yes, I needed glasses.

I remember seeing everything so sharp and clear with the new glasses. I hadn't realized how blurry things had looked to me before. It was incredible seeing the baseball so much more clearly. I didn't want to wear glasses at age fourteen, but I didn't want to be embarrassed not seeing a pop fly again.

I remembered this baseball game so well, because I've always looked back and thought that it was the beginning of my eye disease that threatened to take away my sight completely.

CHAPTER EIGHT

YOU'RE GOING BLIND

My parents noticed that my sister Patty was tripping over objects and running into things. I was fourteen years old and Patty was fifteen at the time. There'd be a toy sitting on the floor in the living room in plain sight and Patty would trip over it. My parents were worried about why she couldn't see where she was going. They took her to Boston for eye tests where she was diagnosed with Usher syndrome (Retinitis Pigmentosa). It is a condition that affects both hearing, vision, and sometimes balance. The symptoms are partial to complete deafness *and* blindness. The nerves deteriorate over time beginning in infancy and continue throughout adulthood. Usher syndrome is a caused by genetic mutations that prevent proteins from maintaining cells in the inner ear and in the retina. Children are often born hard of hearing or deaf and by adolescence they lose peripheral and night vision.

Soon after Patty's diagnosis my parents became concerned about my younger sister Ann and me. They suspected that we also had Usher syndrome. In February 1975, I turned fifteen years old and Ann and I were taken to Massachusetts Eye and Ear Hospital in Boston. The eye tests lasted all day. Pictures were taken of my eyes. It felt like a lightning bolt was flashing inside my eyes with every picture they took. There was also a color test, a dark adaptation test, and an EKG test to see how healthy the rods and cones were in the retina. I remember how I hated that long, dreadful day.

We waited in a tiny lobby for a long time. Then Dr. Berson shared the diagnosis about Ann and me. The news was devasting. In hindsight I didn't fully realize what was going on in the doctor's office, but I remembered seeing my mother's face. She was heartbroken and cried all the way home from Boston. During the quiet drive home Ann and I didn't say anything.

That evening my parents got the family together at the dinner table and shared what happened and gave details about what Dr. Berson told them. Me and my two sisters, Patty and Ann, were all going blind.

I had a hard time believing it. My parents wanted me to accept that I was going blind, but I was into sports, and baseball season was just around the corner. I was also on an ice hockey team. No one was going to tell me I was going blind! I was in shock and angry as well.

I became rebellious about it and continued to pursue my normal day-to-day life and played sports. It was my distraction. Sometimes I would be aware that I had an eye disease when I was playing street hockey if it was getting dark and I couldn't see the orange ball well. I marveled how my friends could see the ball in the dark when I couldn't.

It was hard to accept that I had an eye disease and I tried to ignore the reality. I was in denial. Should my world stop or continue? Should I stay in my bedroom like a sore loser? If my friends asked me if I could see the ball, I would say, "Yeah, let's just play." I watched the other players move around, and I would get an idea of where the ball was rolling. I loved hockey and just couldn't leave the game. Sports was my salvation and a way out of a life-altering situation. I didn't want to tell anyone about my eyesight—so many of my friends did not know.

Being a hearing-impaired teenager and listening to my parents trying to convince me I was going blind was terribly difficult. Every time people said, "you're going blind," it made me feel as if they were saying, *You're going to die. It's the end of the world. You're going to live in a cave all by yourself. No more sports for you!* It was hard for me to accept. I didn't want to hear anything about blindness, since I was still able to see well at the time. My parents were hoping to convince me to think about what I should major in before entering high school, like in data processing. But I was determined to be a designer—blindness and all.

CHAPTER NINE

MOSCOW

I walked into the house from soccer practice and my mom and two sisters, Patty and Ann, were sitting at the dinner table. My mom looked at me so I could see her and said, "Come sit down, I have some big news for you!" I was hoping whatever it was had nothing to do with my blindness. "We're going to Russia this spring because there might be a possible cure or treatment for your eyesight."

I was intrigued about this new adventure, but I wasn't so sure about the cure for our eyes. Still, I was going on a plane to fly across the world to a new and foreign country. I loved the idea of going to Russia because it was a once-in-a-lifetime opportunity. At age fifteen, I didn't believe this cure was real, but I didn't want to go blind either and my parents didn't want my sisters and I to go blind. They made every effort to find a cure for us.

The trip to Russia wasn't easy to arrange because of the Cold War situation with Russia. My mother sought out Senator Ted Kennedy's help to travel to Russia. Apparently it had taken her a lot of work to get permission to go to Russia.

The unusual trip to Russia got a lot of publicity. When I told Mrs. Hopkins at my high school about it, she was thrilled. She knew about my eye disease and she asked, "Is it okay to tell the class about this?"

I never told anyone I had Usher syndrome. Now all my friends and acquaintances would know I was going blind *and* that I was going to Russia with my two sisters for a cure. That created a lot of uncomfortable situations for me. Students began to question me.

"Are you going to become a Communist?"

"Are you a spy?"

"What is the Russian word for 'blind?'"

Some were actually excited for me and some would make fun, acting like a blind person and bumping into me on purpose. I was good natured about it and would laugh along with them. This was high school and being hearing impaired and going blind, I wanted to have friends and get along with everyone. For many it was the first time they learned that I was not only deaf, but also going blind.

I didn't talk much about my eyes, only about the Russian trip. A lot of my friends were more curious about the trip than my impending blindness. That was fine with me, because I didn't want to hear about the thought of going blind. I wanted a bright future, not a blind future.

Many students from high school got involved and raised money to help us pay for our trip to Russia by selling chocolate bars and organizing a fundraising basketball game. The basketball game was the teachers against the students. The local newspaper even advertised the Russian trip and created the Livingston Fund to help my parents pay for our trip. Many donations were made to the fund. Patty and Ann also got into fundraising at their school. Many people from the community, church, and schools gave generously. I was surprised to see many of my friends selling candy bars so that my sisters and I could travel to Russia for treatment. I was extremely grateful for their kindness and generosity.

During my data processing course at the High School, the director from the movie *Jaws* gave me a surprise visit. He wrote a check for the Livingston Fund. Life for me was a bit easier as well because many students were being friendly to me because of this trip—at least for the time being.

Departure Day

At Logan Airport, I stood by the window near the gate.

"It's a 747, Dad!"

He smiled. "I know."

I was finally starting to feel better after a whole day of feeling sick as a dog. I had a stomach flu earlier in the day and I wasn't going to let it stop me from going to Russia. The boarding on the plane was announced and I could never understand announcements being made through a speaker. It was like listening to a dog trying to talk. Me, my two sisters, and my parents hugged all the relatives and friends goodbye. We got on the plane and as it ascended you could see the beautiful city lights of Boston. I was in awe thinking what it was going to be like in Moscow. It felt like I was saying goodbye to the world and going to some alien planet.

I could still see pretty well at that time and when we were over the ocean, I looked out the window and saw the gorgeous, large, round white moon glowing like a pearl, its light shimmering over endless hills and valleys of clouds that stretched out forever. I'd never seen anything so beautiful. I was relaxed and thinking of the people who were at the airport for me and my family. I fell asleep and when I woke up, we were descending and I saw the London clock, Big Ben, passing below.

Being at Heathrow Airport was a strange experience for me. I had never seen so many hippies! There were strange people roaming everywhere in 70s style, with spiky Mohawk haircuts, and strange clothes. There was a huge flight board with rolling lights flashing cities and flights and times, forever changing and foreign voices all around me.

It was like visiting another world, but only for a few hours. Soon we were all hustled back aboard the plane and were pushing down the aisle, settling into our seats. I looked over and there was tennis pro Chris Evert, only twenty-one years old at that time and I wanted to sit with her. I knew who she was, she was pretty, and I wanted to ask her out even though I was only sixteen. Then I realized, *my seat is behind Billie Jean King*! My mother asked Billie Jean King if she was also going to Moscow.

Billie Jean responded with a bit of attitude, saying, "Where else?"

"Well, this plane is also going to Japan," my mother replied giving it right back to Billie Jean.

Billie Jean's husband chuckled.

Then I saw Björn Borg a few seats away. I'm pretty sure it was him, anyway. I figured they were on the way to Moscow for a tennis match. I wasn't that interested because I was more into hockey and baseball.

After a while, the interior got dark, and movie screen turned on up front. For the first time in my life, I saw *The Pink Panther* with Inspector Clouseau. Could life possibly get any better than this? After seeing Clouseau karate–chop Kato out the window I thought that even if the plane crashed in flames I would have died happy.

Many hours later, there was a bump and we landed. We were in Moscow. The heart of the Soviet Union.

After an hour's drive from the airport, we arrived at the Metropol Hotel, tired and hungry. I was also still excited. I was really in Moscow! Stepping out of the car had been like being dropped out of a time machine. Everything was old. I thought big cities were all supposed to look modern. But the cars, the streets, the windows, and the buildings all looked like something out of an old movie from the 1930s or 40s. It was like Gotham from the *Batman* TV shows that I use to watch as a little boy. Many large buildings, like St. Basil's Cathedral off in the distance in Red Square, were many centuries old.

The cars in the streets were round and small or medium–sized, and every one of them was either yellow or black. People on the streets looked gray and grim-faced. There were storefronts with strange, fancy Russian lettering. There were signs and big billboards everywhere covered with hammers and sickles with the same weird but bold script. This was propaganda because May Day, the big Communist celebration, was coming. There were military men in diverse places along the sidewalks.

It was different. It was cool. I loved it!

The Metropol was a short walking distance from Red Square. From the outside, the hotel looked like any other buildings; like something from the 18th century. When we walked in, we looked up to see a huge, colorful dome overhead made of stained glass. There were tall, ornate gold stands like stems that bloomed into massive lamps. And there was a marble fountain in the center of the floor. Live fish swam in it and when guests ordered fish for dinner, the waiters would spear them in the fountain and take them to the cook to be prepared.

A porter met us at the front desk and bundled us into a clear glass elevator that took us up to our rooms. You could look all around and down and see the restaurant and the fountain falling away as you got higher. The rooms themselves were like the rest of the hotel—plush, elegant in a kind of overly fancy way, and years out of date. We unpacked, sneaking looks out the window, trying to catch a glimpse of Red Square and the Kremlin in the distance.

All of us were exhausted and hungry, so we headed to the restaurant, hoping to eat something good. We were interrupted in the hallway by a young guy—tennis pro, Sandy Mayer—who approached my dad. "Do you have a pair of sneakers I could borrow? My luggage seems to have been stolen." Apparently, he needed the sneakers for his tennis practice.

My dad got his sneakers from the hotel room and handed them to Sandy. Then my family and I went to the restaurant and had dinner. It was not easy to order what you wanted. There were no hamburgers and no pizza, but there was plenty of fish. After eating in this elegant restaurant, we all settled in and unpacked.

Later in the evening, Sandy returned the sneakers. By way of thanking my father, he made it a point to get tickets for all of us to see the U.S. team play against the Russians at the Central Lenin Stadium in Moscow. Billie Jean King, Chris Evert, Björn Borg from the USA won easily against the Russians. I was not into tennis, but I had to admit, I had a good time watching Chris Evert!

But I had to remember we weren't tourists. We weren't even patients. We were guinea pigs. We were there for one reason: to get a cure that may or may not change the rest of our lives. Every morning we were supposed to walk to the subway, take the long escalator down to the lower level, and take the train to the Russian hospital where we would be treated.

Before arriving at the clinic for the first time, we had to stop at the embassy to get all the paperwork in order and make it official.

It wasn't easy. Paperwork was a big deal in the Soviet Union and there were a lot of unexpected hassles. When we were all set and ready to go the next morning, the hotel door wouldn't open.

We called the front desk and they sent up someone with a chisel to open it. It made me wonder, *Was this a set–up? Was someone trying to give us a hard time? Did their spy trap break?* Eventually we got out, but I have to say, I had never seen a hotel maintenance man use a chisel on a lock before.

Off we went, walking into an old building with people scowling at us and asking my parents many questions through interpreters and then rubber-stamping papers dozens of times. I remember hearing an old typewriter. I was staring at the woman typing and looking at the keys, which of course had Russian letters on them. It was fascinating for me to watch and learn.

Eventually we were assigned a guide and interpreter from Intourist, a Communist travel agency that was there to show us around. *Was our guide KGB?* I didn't care; he was nice. But my parents were cautious. We were told that we were to take the subway each morning to the hospital and then come back to the hotel after the treatments.

We had gone from watching *The Pink Panther* on screen to living in a James Bond movie in real life. How cool was that? I was having fun exploring. So far, the trip had been a lot of fun for me. However, it would have been better if they'd served pizza and it was hard getting used to the food.

The next morning, we were ready to travel to the hospital for our first treatment. We went to the subway, the Metro, which was astonishing; a long, underground golden palace. The crowds were insane.

People were looking at us as we descended on the escalator, moved into the crowds, and then squeezed into the subway car. I remember hearing the Russian announcer speaking in Russian before the door closed. All the Russians stared at us because we were wearing colorful jackets and were obviously Americans. I wore a bright yellow sports jacket. No one in Russia wore yellow or pretty much any other color. The clothes were like the buildings and the grey sky—like how it would look if I were color blind.

We got off the train and walked a short way toward our destination.

When we finally got to the hospital, well, let's say it wasn't what we were expecting, even by Russian standards. Before the hospital became a hospital, it had been a police station, and the feeling of bars and inter-rogation rooms lingered like a heavy smell. In fact, there *was* a heavy smell. The floor was old, all the walls were tiled, and patients sat in decrepit seats in the corridors outside the examination rooms.

Worst of all was the bathroom. To reach it, you had to take the stairs to the first level and go down. There were no doors on the stalls. There was no toilet paper; you had to bring your own! I avoided using the bathroom. I told myself to just wait till I got back to the hotel.

The procedure itself wasn't too bad. The doctor came in and after a lengthy eye examination I waited for the nurse who then waved me into a small cell. She brought out a long needle and gave me the shot. At first, I was a little nervous because I had no idea what to expect. I kept asking myself, *where am I getting my shot? What should I do? Would I understand her?* But it was all simple; a piece of cake.

My sisters and I were given two shots a day for twenty-one days. After that first examination, the routine was pretty quick. The doctor would come by, look at me, take some notes, give me the shot, and that was that. I hated having to wait between shots, the first shot was at 9 a.m. and the second shot was at 3 p.m. We had to wait patiently between treatments. The doctors and their assistants were kind people. The nurses knew a little English and made conversation with me. Their bro-ken English was like my broken ears and we communicated using gestures or pointed to pictures in a book. I was able to understand some of the things the nurse would say. For instance, the nurse showed me a picture of New York and I was assuming she was asking me if I've been to New York. "No, but I'm from Boston," I said.

"Boston, da," she said with a smile.

It wasn't hard to read people in Russia since I had always observed nonverbal communications growing up hearing-impaired. Expressions are important when observing.

In the beginning, it felt as though we were there all day. It wasn't what I had dreamed of coming thousands of miles to see.

At the end of the day, we went back to the hotel where dinner was waiting. The doctor told us to stay away from tomato sauce and chocolate, but that wasn't a problem; pizzas and chocolate were not on the menu. It was mostly fish and then ice cream for dessert. While everyone was eating there was a stage with entertainers singing American tunes every night. My mother would tell us what song they were playing.

Over dinner I started to get to know the Russian people. I didn't know or care anything about politics, but I know when people are grateful or work hard or like the same things you do. There was no tipping, but the Intourist guide said I could share my gum with people, so I gave my waiters some American gum to say thanks. They were overwhelmed; incredibly touched. I brought my sports magazines to the table, and when I saw the waiters peeking a look, I knew they had an interest in sports. I saw it in their eyes and their gestures, so I gave them my copies. They were as crazy about sports as I was, and you couldn't miss the genuine appreciation, or the extra–nice service they gave in return. The staff in the rooms, too—they couldn't have worked harder. If you threw your shirt on the bed, you'd find them in the bathroom cleaning it on a washboard. After realizing this, I had to put my clothes in the drawer.

After dinner, I had a chance now and then to go out. My family and I walked the streets, watching the soldiers marching by Lenin's Tomb and looking up at Saint Basil's Cathedral with those famous domes. We saw the hammer and sickle everywhere. The day would come when the place would be more open to the West, but back then, it was like going back in time.

We did some shopping, too. There was a big store that was called GUM. It was like the Quincy Market in Boston. There were lots of people shopping and browsing.

I was amazed at how many Russian people knew English. Some spoke broken English with whom I identified with because of my hearing-impairment.

It would have been nice to be able to speak Russian at the restaurant, because sometimes I wanted to order food I saw being served at other tables. The menu had some English on it, but every time I pointed to what I wanted, it came out disappointing. The waiters were not good with nonverbal communications so I decided to stick with fish. They had no trouble when I pointed to fish.

Even though the trip was stressful and lengthy, we left with many good memories of the restaurants, the sights, the people, and the adventure of it all.

After staying in Russia for three weeks, we took a flight from Moscow to Poland and finally to Boston, Massachusetts. The interesting thing about traveling to another country is that when you come back, you appreciate the life you have at home. I don't think I ever appreciated America more. A lot of students were interested in knowing what happened in Russia. So, for a couple of weeks, I was highly appreciated at my high school and I had plenty of stories to tell everyone.

The only way I can describe the effect of the shots is that my vision seemed brighter or clearer; more normal. I told the doctors in Boston about it, but they dismissed it. They said the trip had gotten our hopes up and that we were imagining things. When they tested us, they didn't find any improvement to our vision, but it was too soon to tell if the vaccine was halting the disease. I even thought I heard some sounds from the headset on the airplane, but I realized I was deceiving myself believing that I was hearing better.

I had mixed feelings about the Russian vaccine. I asked myself, *was it worth getting forty-two shots?* I thought it was the adventure of going to Russia that kept me going. I was not afraid being part of the Cold War even though I never really paid attention to politics. Politics created fear in people and I wanted freedom to see a new country. Back at home people feared my deafness because they didn't know how to communicate with me or simply judged me. Some people would think I couldn't function in the hearing world because they didn't want to try. What they didn't realize is that I was easy to communicate with. I was looking forward to positive changes that the vaccine might do, hoping my hearing and eyesight would get better. Hope was my savior until one day that changed my life forever.

CHAPTER TEN

THE SILENCE

About a month after coming back to America from the first of three trips to Russia, I was playing street hockey with my friends from the neighborhood in a vacant parking lot, where you didn't have to worry about breaking a car window. I still wore my hearing aid on my left ear as usual. I never wore a hearing aid in my right ear because it never responded to any sounds. I probably had no hearing in my right ear since birth. After I finished playing a game, I stopped at an apartment duplex of one of my friends I'd been playing with. Steve and I went into his kitchen. It had an old-fashion rotary telephone mounted on the wall. I needed to call my mother, so I switched my hearing aid to telephone mode. I picked up the phone and then dialed her at home. My mother picked it up after the first ring and we started to talk. And then, suddenly I couldn't hear her voice anymore. Not a sound. Nothing.

Silence.

Puzzled, I gave the phone to my friend. "Is there something wrong with the phone? My mom is on the other end. Can you hear her?" I realized I couldn't even hear my own voice either. Something was terribly wrong.

I switched my hearing aid back to microphone normal setting and I still could not hear any sound, my friend talking, or my own voice.

I watched him he put the phone to his ear and mouthed the word, "Hello?"

He could hear her, he mouthed back to me.

"I can't hear anything," I said.

I guessed my mother overheard me from the phone. She explained to my friend that maybe the hearing aid batteries had died, or maybe it was broken.

I watched my friend's lips move as he told me what she said, and I understood it. But I couldn't hear him. I couldn't hear anything. I began to sweat with fear of going deaf. I panicked.

Silently, I sat on the sidewalk curb, waiting for my mom to pick me up. When she arrived, I got in the car and lip–read her saying, "Maybe it's the wax in your ear. We'll go to the hospital to check it out right away, since you had this wax build up in your ear before."

The doctors at the hospital cleaned out my ear, and still I couldn't hear. The hearing aid was checked out and working fine; they said it was making its dreadful whistling noise, as usual. The next day, we visited Dr. Arrigg, my audiologist, and I had a hearing test. Dr. Arrigg gave us the bad news that I was totally deaf and that there was nothing to be done about it. Nothing!

I sat in silence. Stunned by the news.

I didn't take it well. I was sixteen. I was *stone* deaf and going blind. My world ended that day and I couldn't focus, because as soon as I woke up that morning, I was having a bad attack of tinnitus, a persistent ringing in my ears. It was so severe and sounded like a jet engine roaring constantly in my head. It made me sick and dizzy for three days after I lost all my hearing. It was a horrible three days.

I was fortunate that I could lipread well and could speak well. These abilities would help me because I was unprepared for the sudden impact of going completely deaf.

I had to move on. I knew I had to deal with it. I consoled myself that from now on I wouldn't have to wear hearing aids anymore, or even see my audiologist again.

What was the point? I was completely deaf!

I felt free of the difficult hearing aids, but I hated the silence. It was like watching a television show without the sound on. Closed captioning didn't even exist at that time. It drove me crazy not being able to hear the TV. I had to learn to adjust to total silence. I started depending more on vibrations and imitating them. I probably ended up developing a deeper voice. Feeling the vibration of a stereo speaker made me feel a little better. I would imitate and create my own sounds by feeling vibrations from the hands and neck. I also became more dependent on my sense of smell, touch, and feel, and what remained of my deteriorating vision. The last songs I remembered listening to were by Seals and Crofts and John Denver. I could feel the beats of "Diamond Girl" on the speaker but I couldn't feel anything from the John Denver album because it was more verbal. I missed the 70s music, but I kept playing the songs in my head so I wouldn't forget how much I loved music.

I felt I was thrown into a dark cave. The silence made me lonelier than ever. I started to wonder about my future and how I would manage being deaf and blind for the rest of my life. The thought was terrifying. I became depressed thinking about a dark future.

Eventually, I stopped thinking about the future and moved on. I said to myself, *I am going to be like anyone else anyway and there's no stopping me.*

CHAPTER ELEVEN

I ONLY ASKED TO BE FREE

I started my sophomore year in high school as a totally deaf person, but I was stubborn to admit it. My school counselor would tell me that I should learn sign language, but the problem was that no one knew sign language at my school. Not even my own family or friends knew it. My dad tried to encourage me to learn it, but I didn't want to. I felt it would disconnect me from the hearing world. I didn't see any point learning how to sign.

"Who am I going to sign to?" I asked my counselor. "Myself?"

The counselor didn't know anything about using an interpreter either. I got to know a deaf man in my neighborhood who couldn't speak well. He invited me to a deaf club in downtown Lawrence, Massachusetts which hosted a social gathering and a movie night. During the socials I couldn't understand any of them because they were all communicating in sign language. They were watching a movie called, *Butterflies Are Free* filmed in 1972 and it was subtitled, which I had never seen before and thought it was really cool. Ironically, the movie was about a blind man who wanted to get away from his mother and live on his own and ended up falling in love with a young woman.

The whole experience of the deaf club was different and new to me, a culture shock. After the movie I got uncomfortable and decided the whole deaf scene wasn't for me and I wanted to leave. They encouraged me to come back again. But I was trying to deal with the sudden loss of my hearing. I didn't want anything to do with deaf people and learning sign language wasn't for me.

I was sixteen years old with a rebellious attitude. I came so far to be part of a hearing world since the day that I stepped out of the audiology booth with a radio strapped to my chest. I had been involved in sports and activities. I had many hearing friends through good times and bad times, and I fought and worked hard to be with the hearing. How could I surrender to a deaf world in a day? I was an extroverted person and outgoing. I was determined that nothing would stop me from living in the hearing world.

I realized there was a humorous side to be deaf. Throughout high school social events, people would assume I was hearing, because I had the ability to use my voice. Sometimes it was a problem because they argued with me.

"You can hear me Woody. Knock it off. What are you, deaf?"

In some ways this was a compliment. I had a stubborn mindset about some of these dumb people who yelled at me and I enjoyed having the last few choice words with them when I told them I was totally deaf.

When I met new people, usually I would tell them that I lipread well and that I was deaf. Sometimes they would raise their voice and I would be able to tell by their expressions.

"Do you have to yell?" I asked. "Do you know what it means when you can't hear a sound?"

"Yes!" they would say even louder, veins popping out of their neck and forehead.

"Then why were you yelling?" I would ask.

Most of my high school teachers did not understand deafness either. This was the 1970s and they were clueless. Many didn't understand that I needed to lipread them to follow what they were saying. They would talk in class and walk around the classroom into positions where I wasn't able to lipread them. Getting an education was frustrating and difficult to say the least.

One day, I was sitting in English class with my friend Sue. The teacher was writing on the blackboard and talking.

"What was she saying?" I asked Sue. I couldn't lipread her facing the blackboard.

"Do you mind telling the class what you and Woody were talking about?" the teacher turned and yelled at Sue.

"I was telling Woody what you were saying."

"Well, he should be listening to me," the teacher snapped back.

"Well, he would be, but he's deaf," Sue said and rolled her eyes.

The teacher grew red with anger, stomped her foot, and then continued writing on the board.

When I had my hearing aid it was a little easier to pick up a few words, but when I was totally deaf most teachers didn't want to deal with it. I couldn't help but become resentful at the blatant neglect I was experiencing. I would try to get help from some of the girls in class because they were good writers and they would share their notes with me. A few people thought I was taking advantage of the girls. I didn't like relying on people for notes, but I needed it to survive. Because most of my teachers didn't care to help me, it was a big effort in almost every class to figure out who I could rely on for notes.

Every Friday my social studies teacher would give a verbal bonus question to the class, which was completely unfair to me. It was impossible to understand what he was saying. I didn't like him, because he didn't care that I was deaf. "I'm not wasting my time with you!" he once told me.

"You're supposed to be a teacher? Yikes." I retorted, angry and frustrated beyond belief.

"Get out of my classroom," he said his eyes enraged.

I happily got up and walked out and yelled after him, "Screw you!" I knew that he couldn't do anything about it because what he said in front of the class could get him in trouble with administration.

When I returned to my social studies class things got even worse. At first it seemed like everything was fine and forgotten. Later in my first class back I was doing my handouts at my desk. A student who sat behind me began messing around and kicked my seat. Of course, I asked him to stop, but he kicked my chair again so hard that I fell to the floor. The teacher got upset as I sat stunned on the floor. He grabbed me by the shirt and threw me out of the classroom. He knew the other student did it but singled me out. I realized then he didn't like me because I was deaf. Maybe at one point in his life he had a deaf uncle who was mean to him or his dog went deaf and he was taking it out on me. Who knows?

I wanted to tell Mrs. Hopkins or the principal, but I didn't know how or if they would help me. I was afraid of retribution. Finally, I was able to transfer to another class with a better teacher. The experience taught me that some adults were as bad as the students who picked on me.

Silence Isn't So Golden After All...

I soon learned that there were even more challenges being totally deaf in a hearing world. When I was hard of hearing, I could hear the school bell, heard half the things the teachers were saying and heard the roars and cheers during sports. Being totally deaf was depressing and full of perils. It was a battle to stay alive in a jungle full of wild animals— silent crocodiles who kicked you out of their class for being deaf, inaudible chimpanzees who kicked your seat out from under you for being deaf, and rattlesnakes who didn't rattle and yelled at the top of their lungs telling you that you couldn't succeed in their world. The funny thing, in my freshman year in high school, students used to pick on me for wearing a hearing aid but by my sophomore year, the teachers and adults were bigger problems than the students, my peers, and my friends. Being completely deaf, I made more friends than I did with my hearing aid. I didn't let anything stop me. I think most students and a few teachers liked my enthusiasm as a deaf person, because I tried so hard and played many sports and activities.

Back to Russia...With Love

We were supposed to go back every six months. It took about a year before we went back to Russia for the second round of treatments and I was happy to go. It meant no homework for three weeks and a minor break from the difficult and sometimes mean-spirited social life I had to endure at school.

After I lost my hearing completely, I had wondered whether the first trip caused my total deafness. No one really seemed to know. In hindsight it was an experimental treatment; there were always risks. The doctors looked at the charts and papers, had discussions with my parents, and didn't see any reasons to stop me and my sisters from going back to Moscow for more treatments. I went back to Russia totally deaf and I worried about what would happen after the second trip. Would I lose all my vision? We were guinea pigs after all. But to me, the potential reward was greater than the risk.

In January 1977, we boarded a plane for Moscow. It was much easier than our first time. There were no reporters or crowds at the airport, and it was so much quieter. My mother didn't come this time, which meant less luggage, less paperwork, and less parental supervision. We knew the routine; where and how to take the subway, what to eat, and who to talk to. This time we stayed at the Berlin Hotel.

Because it was late January, it was much colder than during the first trip. I didn't think it was as cold as many people made it out to be; it wasn't like it was the North Pole. It was good to be in Moscow in January just to get a taste of what winter was really like in Russia. I had been to Rochester, New York before and I thought the weather was similar; snow flurries and cloudy for seven out of ten days.

Since I was totally deaf at the time, I had to use my eyes and other senses more. I had difficulty lipreading Russians with speaking English with heavy accents. My dad did most of the talking.

We were there for twenty-one days, and I didn't care who was watching us. I would be spending my seventeenth birthday in Moscow. I wanted to invite a lot of people to the hotel restaurant and have a big party like the wedding I saw on the first trip, but I knew it wasn't going to happen.

Every day, we found ourselves in the same old former police station, waiting between injections. Sometimes we would go back to the hotel in between. My dad and I would play games of chess; which I liked because I had been on the chess club when I went to Bruce School. My sisters would listen to music or do crossword puzzles. I couldn't hear the 1970s music that my sister was always playing on her cassette recorder. No music was a major downside to being deaf. I missed music in a big way. It made me think that I would rather be totally blind than totally deaf.

Every day we passed women sweeping snow from the sidewalks and we gave them a friendly smile. We did a lot of walking and saw other hardworking people on the streets. I liked the idea of walking through the underground crosswalks at busy intersections. I thought it was convenient for blind people. You didn't have to worry about crossing busy intersections and possibly getting hit by a car.

It was our routine to walk every day and then get our shots, forty-two in total for the three weeks. It wouldn't have been so bad if I had been doing this by myself because I could have been sightseeing and exploring the area in between the daily shots. This was Russia during the Cold War though, and we had to be cautious.

When my friends from school told me how bad Russia was, I would ask if they had actually been there. I made sure to tell them that the Russians were friendly and hardworking people; there was no reason to hate or fear them. Politics could be deceiving.

We were able to do a few fun things before the trip was over. We went to see the ballet at the Bolshoi Theatre, which was within walking distance, and we saw the Bolshoi Circus, a popular event in Moscow.

After saying goodbye to the people at the hospital we took a flight from Moscow to Switzerland and flew over the magnificent Alps. While the plane was descending and zig–zagging the view was breathtaking. I wanted to reach out and touch those mountains.

My eyes were still good enough back then to see those mountains. I decided on that flight that no one was going to tell me I was going blind. I wasn't going to worry about my future. I had to live one day at a time.

When we arrived in Boston, no crowds were waiting for us. I went back to school and back to some of the same frustrations that never seemed to end. I loved varsity baseball, but my coach had not been nice to me. It didn't matter if I got a hit, stole a base, or played well. During one game, the coach needed a player for left field. One of my teammates suggested, "put Woody in."

"I don't want a deaf guy," the coach snickered,

I had read his lips and understood what he said. I was angry and wanted to punch him, but of course I restrained myself. I quit baseball and moved on. I didn't want to be around a guy like that and I didn't want to have any situations with him like I had with the social studies teacher. When I played soccer or ran indoor track, I was always competitive. I won races and became a starter for the varsity soccer team which made some people jealous. There was one boy who started picking on me after he didn't make the varsity soccer team. He would gesture in a silly way as if he was a deaf person which was irritating. I vented about it to my favorite teacher, Mrs. Hopkins who was always understanding and kind.

In December that year another obnoxious kid was sitting right next to me in front of the substitute teacher in geometry class. He kept hitting the back of my head.

"You'd better stop!" I barked at him.

Then he ripped my clip tie off my neck. I was so angry and punched him right in the face and knocked him off his seat. I had had enough.

The substitute teacher panicked and didn't know what to do. She ran out of class to get help so I grabbed the bloody–nosed kid and said to him, "Do that one more time and I'll punch you again. Knock it off!"

Of course, we were both called to the principal's office. Mrs. Hopkins was there. "We're going to give you a Christmas gift," she said with her hands on her hips. "You won't be suspended. I'm sorry no one stopped that kid sooner."

I knew violence wasn't the answer, but I was fortunate that Mrs. Hopkins knew about the harassment I was receiving from other students. I learned it was better to talk about my issues with other people I trusted. I loved that woman. She was the only one who understood my frustrations. She had my back and went out of her way to prevent me from getting into any more trouble. I didn't want it be a burden on her though. I had many good friends, but there were even more bad kids. It was time I stood up for myself and the more I stood up, the more fights I got into. During my junior and senior years, I grew taller, stronger, and even tougher.

The stark reality of having to defend myself was not lost on me one day when I was on my way to English class. A girl walked by and smiled at me and I said "hi." Suddenly, a guy stalked me from behind and sucker punched me in the face. I had no idea what happened and thought, *what the heck?* I dropped all my books and beat him so badly that one of my good friends had to stop me. He patted me on the back and pulled off the student.

I gathered my books and walked through the crowds milling around. Who had seen the whole thing? Luckily no teachers were around. When I walked into my English class my friends were high-fiving me. "Why did that kid punch me?" I asked my friend Darrell. I was furious.

"He was jealous of you, because that was his girlfriend you smiled at," he said.

Mr. Burns, my English teacher then walked in. He looked at me like he knew what had just happened. "Hey Woody! Got any news for me?"

Rather than tell him about what happened in the hallway I pulled out a *National Enquirer* article and handed it to him. I asked Mr. Burns to read it to the class because they'd get a good kick out of it. The cover predicted that aliens were coming to America and all women would become bald. The Mr. Burns and the whole class could not stop laughing.

Laughter was good medicine for me. It displaced anger inside me and eased my frustration.

Humor also helped me reset and take in the good things that were happening in my life. I realized I was becoming a good lipreader. When people were open and nice to me, it gave me a chance to learn and it helped me avoid people who were toxic.

The Final Trip to Moscow

During my junior year of high school, we took our third and final trip to Russia. This time, we stayed at the Metropol again which was nice. There was a piano in one of our rooms but I didn't much care for it. With the low keys I could feel the vibrations but with the high pitch keys I couldn't. All I would play were the low pitch keys that would probably drive a hearing person crazy! I also learned that if you didn't want the Russians eavesdropping you played the piano!

The routine was much easier this final time in Russia. It was less of a hassle because we were used to some of the Russian food by then. The only problem was getting the orders right. My dad once told the waiter that he wanted five ice creams for dessert; showing five fingers. The waiter nodded as if he knew what he meant. The waiter returned and delivered five ice creams for each of us! I enjoyed my second straight birthday in Moscow and I didn't mind eating all five ice creams!

The Taste of Freedom

When you're an American and you bolt out of a Moscow hotel during the height of the Cold War with no passport and no identification, it was possible you could disappear. But I wasn't thinking of that. I only wanted to be free. Just like that, I walked out of the hotel room. I wanted downtime to be alone. I had become an eighteen-year-old adult and I wanted a taste of freedom. I hit the elevator button, got to the first floor, and walked out past the Metropol doors into the street of Moscow. I slipped into the Russian crowds and was gone.

I walked aimlessly for blocks. There was nothing to fear. Occasionally I would see a Russian civilian or soldier looking at me. I wore my bright red sports jacket and it just shouted "American." But when I looked back, they ignored me.

I came upon a park. There were patches of snow everywhere, and there was a wrought iron bench by the path that looked out over a large pond that was frozen. Birds flew around the pond and perched on the chunks of ice. I sat on the bench and looked around. *Where is this place? What have I gotten myself into? What should I do now? How will I get back?* For a moment I thought, *Do I even want to get back?*

I was eighteen. I could make my own choices. Russia was so big, so strange, so closed off from the rest of the world. Why couldn't I just get lost in it? I could stay here. It wouldn't be the American life I was living at home. But for one crazy moment I could feel freedom—my complete freedom. All I needed to do was to take a step in any direction that would lead to a totally different future. A whole new life. I had a choice to make about my life.

A man wearing the usual heavy coat and fur hat walked up the path and joined me. He sat down to catch his breath. He was dressed like an old Cossack. Like most Russians he had a wide, friendly face, and a ready smile. He tried to strike up a conversation, but since I couldn't hear and he didn't speak English, it didn't go anywhere. He smiled anyway and nodded knowingly. We sat there together for a while. A Cossack from a distant past and a young man from the present.

I always kept some gum in my pocket because I knew Russians liked American gum. Gum was extremely expensive in Russia and I liked to hand it out as a tip or as a thank you gift or as a way to break the ice. I once gave a stick to an elderly Russian woman who began to eat the wrapper and all.

I rummaged in my pocket and pulled out a package of gum. Sure enough, there was a stick left, and also a business card from the Metropol. I offered the old Cossack the stick of gum.

He took it and nodded his thanks. Then he noticed the Metropol card. He pointed at the card and gestured in a direction. *That way to the hotel.*

I thanked him for the information.

We sat together for a while longer. Then I got up and waved good-bye and headed back in the direction of the hotel.

I was free, wasn't I? I had wanted to be out and on my own. I didn't care how long it lasted. I was free if only for a moment and I was doing it In Russia. My sisters wouldn't dare do that. People would tell me constantly that I was crazy. I didn't care what they thought. I did it, and that's all that mattered to me. I walked around the streets, looked at the people, at the small, old, black and yellow cars, looked up at the old buildings, and I went where I felt like going, on my own. Independent. Getting along just fine.

After a while, I figured I should be getting back to my family.

All my life, people have wanted to protect me from the world, and all my life I've wanted to experience it in my own way and on my own terms. I wanted to escape, and I had, and I knew now that I could do so again anytime I wanted. Deaf, blind, or not, on the other side of the world or not, I had been out on the town on my own and I was content. I had tasted freedom and I knew I was ready to go out on my own.

After completing three trips to Moscow, the doctor in Boston, Dr. Berson, gave me a completed check-up when I got back. He confirmed that there was no change in my eyesight. He suggested not going back to Russia, since he did not believe the treatment was working or halting the disease.

That was okay. It was time to move on and not worry about a cure. Thinking about a cure was deceptive, sometimes false hope. I was glad I wasn't really expecting a cure while in Russia. Learning that it did not work would have probably made me depressed or discouraged. Sometimes going to Massachusetts Eye and Ear was deceiving enough. It raised my hope only to dash it. I would look at the results and it seemed more dire than it really was. I once told the doctor that I didn't think the results were as accurate as it said. The results said I could only see one-hundredth of normal vision at night.

Dr. Berson wanted to prove me wrong. "I'm going to dim the lights and you tell me how many fingers the woman across the room is showing you."

He dimmed the lights low and had the woman signal with her fingers. I was able to read every number she signaled. Dr. Berson was amused. "I stand corrected."

And with that I was able to convince him my eyes were good enough to drive.

CHAPTER TWELVE

ON MY OWN

After the last Russian trip, I wanted to experience being on my own. I was determined and eighteen years old. After I finished my junior year in high school, I worked a summer job as a carpenter. I loved it and was inspired to build my own home someday. I actually liked carpentry better than the commercial art I was doing in school.

I saved my money over the summer for a motorcycle because I was into dirt biking through the trails in the woods. I moved into a studio apartment on my own when I started my senior year in high school. It wasn't easy. I worked night shifts at a fancy restaurant in Lawrence, which was nice because I was able to have dinner there for free on my working days. I also met a few professional hockey players from the Boston Bruins. I used to sneak out of the kitchen to get their autographs while they were finishing up their meal.

I didn't have any deafness discrimination issues and the supervisor appreciated having me work for him. I didn't have to hear to be a dishwasher or to go in and out of the kitchen to collect all the dirty dishes from the tables. The only issue I was having was that the restaurant was dark, and I was starting to have night vision issues. I had to be cautious. It was like wearing a pair of sunglasses. I didn't want anyone knowing I had an eye disease or receive any special treatment for it either.

It was difficult to keep up with my schedule. I went to work right after school and finished just before 11 p.m. I would drive my motorcycle back to my studio apartment in Methuen and crash in bed and sometimes I would get up late and end up going to school late. I learned the hard way; life wasn't easy.

Since I had a studio apartment on the ground level, I used to sneak the motorcycle into the apartment so that no one would steal it. It got too cold to ride a motorcycle in the late fall.

The funny thing about having a studio apartment in my senior year in high school was I had to figure out how I was going to wake up in the morning for school. Since I couldn't hear an alarm clock, I plugged in a hair dryer into a timer. I had the hair dryer start up at 6 a.m. on my headboard and blow air on my head. It usually worked well for me. There were times the hair dryer would fall off the headboard and I would miss the bus and I would drive my motorcycle to school.

I only lasted three months living at the studio apartment and then ended up staying with friends nearer to the school.

I took a driving course that year and got my driver's license. My eyes were still pretty good during the day, but I did start to lose some peripheral vision, and I was cautious. I drove the driver's education teacher crazy because I wanted to drive all over the place and she had a hard time getting my attention to follow instructions because I couldn't hear her and I was focused on paying attention to the road. After completing this course, she gave me a hug. "I could never stay upset with you because you're such a handsome man," she said and then handed me my certificate.

That winter I stayed at a friend's house near the Merrimac River. The high school was directly across the river. I had always wanted to skate across the river with my friend Ken. We put on our skates and stepped out onto the ice, skating slowly to check for cracks.

We barely got ten feet out when the ice started cracking. "No way I'm crossing the river," Ken said.

"Come on," I dared him. "You'll be late for school. "You would have to walk two miles to the bridge"

"No way!"

I decided I was going to race across the thin ice.

Before I turned to take off, Ken yelled, "You're crazy; you're going to drown!"

I didn't care. I wanted to beat the odds rather than listen to another person telling me I couldn't do something. I took a deep breath and off I went. I skated across the river as fast as I could. I felt the ice cracking and the water rising and I was splashing water with my skates but made it across the wide river scared and shivering. I looked across the river and Ken was waving.

"I made it!" I laughed.

When I turned behind me I saw the path I skated through. The ice was all broken up. I realized I could have drowned and never did it again. But at least I didn't have to walk two miles to school that day like Ken did.

Boxing

My friend Ronnie from my Commercial Arts class told me about a boxing center that had just opened up next door to his house on Water Street. I was desperate to try new things that year so I joined Ronnie in taking up boxing. After training there for a week, Joe the instructor was trying to figure a way to communicate with me while boxing.

"When the bell rings, I will tag you on your back so you can start the bout."

My first bout I was boxing with a kid who had been there for over a year. As soon as the first round started I punched and jabbed the kid so many times that I never gave him a chance to punch back. I knocked him down fast. By the look on Joe's face he was surprised that I had defeated the kid so easily.

"Are you a street fighter?" he asked as I got out of the ring.

"Sometimes I get into fights."

"Once you're trained, you're going to be a good boxer!"

I smiled in confusion, thinking to myself, *I don't want to be a boxer.*

A month later, I had a bout with another amateur boxer, and he was a pretty good one. I finished him off in the first round with a knock-out.

When I got down from the ring, Ronnie came over, "Wow, you knocked the crap out of that kid, he was supposed to be a gold glove boxer!"

Joe kept telling me I was going to be a professional, but I still wasn't sure I wanted to keep boxing.

The following week, Joe sent an older, heavier man into the ring to box with me. "He is going to kill me," I told Joe. "He looks like a pro!"

"Don't worry, if you can get through three rounds, then you're ready for professional bouts."

I was nervous. The guy looked ten years older than me. I fought him for the first three minute round that felt more like ten. I was completely exhausted. While I sat in my corner I looked at Ron and lipread him.

"You're doing great, but don't piss him off!"

I laughed. This would be my first time going into the second round because I had knocked out guys in the first round of my other bouts. The second round was as hard as the first. My opponent jabbed me hard, so I started punching at him hard and by the end of the second round, I gave the guy a good jab in the face, hoping he would fall but the bell rang, and he was fine.

Again, I sat in the corner with Joe coaching me to keep my arms close together. I looked over at Ronnie again who laughed, "You're pissing him off!"

I ignored him. I was exhausted and drained. I didn't think I had any energy left to finish the third and final round. When the bell rang I saw that my opponent didn't even look exhausted. We fought the whole round and he couldn't knock me down. I was so exhausted. When it ended Joe told me I did great.

I looked at Ronnie once more time. "I guess he wasn't pissed off enough," he said exaggerating his lip movements.

I shoved at Ronnie with a laugh.

"Are you ready for your first bout next month?" Joe asked.

"I don't know if I want to box anymore."

Afterwards, I was in a weightlifting and arm-wrestling tournament. I actually won an arm-wrestling tournament at the Boys Club. A lot of guys treated me with respect after winning that championship. I felt so good that it eased my anger at the world. But at that age, I couldn't stick to one thing, I wanted to explore everything. I got bored with boxing but it was a good experience for me to show that a deaf person can box. I've always thought being totally deaf helped me concentrate on certain things without any noise distractions. I could look at the opponent's expression to see if he had fear or exhaustion dripping from his eyes; a good time to knock him down.

Through my senior year, I missed quite a few days, but my grades were still good. I made sure to take advantage of the easy courses.

Later in the year I interviewed for a job in silk screening but having to smell the chemicals and working with paint was not what I wanted to do. I turned it down and asked the manager if he would give the job to my friend Sue, who was also in my major, and was with me to assist me as a lipreading interpreter.

Sue was easy to lipread and comfortable to talk to. I wasn't sure if I would understand the interviewer, but it turned out I could understand him well. Sue took the offer. I was disappointed that this was not what I expected, but I was happy for Sue. Mrs. Hopkins had set up that job interview for me to work at after high school.

Considering a career started me thinking about college and I immediately applied to a local community college, hoping I was not too late. As a deaf person, there were many things that misdirected me—mainly people failing to communicate with me.

There were optional lectures about college careers, how to apply to colleges, and programs to find out what you wanted to accomplish in life. But I missed those lectures and I had no idea of what I wanted to do. My friends hadn't clued me into what was going on, because they were competing against me. I didn't have a realistic understanding of what I wanted to do.

Commercial arts was a fun major, but I didn't like the job market for it. I didn't care for the graphic design part that was required in my senior year. I was good at painting letters and numbers on classroom doors as a co-op, but I hated it. I couldn't figure out what I wanted to do, but I knew it wasn't graphic design or anything having to do with paint. I graduated high school in four years and the war was over!

The principal made sure to approach me on my graduation day after the ceremony was over. He looked at me and took me by the shoulders. "You were a piece of work," he said and gave me a hug.

CHAPTER THIRTEEN

ESCAPED

After high school I was confused about my future. I had many friends and some had not been a good influence. I became wild and outgoing. It was as if I had a death wish. Some of my friends wanted to hang out with me because I was entertaining to be around with fast cars, dirt biking, and going to the beach with girls. I could not sit still; I always had to be active, especially on weekends.

That summer, I worked for an outreach program, landscaping along the Merrimac River. On a Friday, at my boss's office downtown Lawrence, I went to pick up my paycheck and ended up talking to the secretary who was working there. I was telling her that I was waiting to hear from Northern Essex Community College, hoping for an acceptance letter. It was getting to be too late to enroll.

"Oh, my boyfriend works at the administration office," she said with a chipper smile.

"Can you call him and put in a word for me?" I asked. "I'm deaf, I cannot hear the phone"

"Oh sure, I'll call him right now!"

"Hi Hon, there's a gentleman who is deaf," she said. Watching her speak, I imagined that she had an elegant voice that matched her pretty face. "His name is Woody Livingston and he's waiting for an acceptance letter. Can you look into it?"

She hung up the phone and told me to stay five minutes. I waited for ten and the phone rang because I noticed that she picked up the headset.

"Uh huh, ok, I'll tell him."

She hung up the phone. "You're all set," she said. "He will send you the acceptance letter today!"

I was thrilled to be going to college, hoping it would lead me somewhere. After the first week, I realized that college was a much faster pace than high school. Going to college for the first time was confusing because of my deafness. I couldn't understand the professors well in class. I had no idea what was happening. One of my professors told me that there was a note–taking service. I had to request a note-taker from the handicapped support services office.

The office was small with a little lounge that could seat four people with a table in the middle. I walked into the office. Ruben, the counselor was sitting at his desk and looked up. "Hi," he said with a friendly smile. "You must be Woody."

We quickly became friends. He found a note-taker for all of my classes. It helped enough that I was able to pass my courses. But I wasn't satisfied that I could pass the courses because I wasn't understanding everything. I was memorizing the definition of a word, but not understanding the meaning.

When I took accounting, I struggled hard because I didn't understand the words the professor was saying. The professor met up with me after class and told me she could tell that I was frustrated.

"It isn't fair that you're working so hard on the assignments and missing out on the details I've been teaching. It would be so much easier if you could hear, because you would do well."

"There must be a solution," I replied.

But unfortunately, she was speechless and had nothing more to say on the matter.

I was discouraged, but I continued to move on. I only took a few courses and worked at night for a company that made plastic garbage bags. I was confused. I wanted a real job, one that would require the use of my brain, not just my hands. At times, I would work at the Boys Club after class. The Boys Club was a good influence on me and I liked the owner, Jack. He was a great guy.

I had a great deal of free time while I was in college and had lots of friends who constantly wanted to go out. One day, I decided to walk home and a friend, Don, yelled and waved out of his car as he was driving by. "Let me take you home Woody!" So, I joined him.

He was yelling in excitement about his car.

"Why are you yelling?" I asked.

"I forgot, you can't hear anything," he said with a laugh. People often forgot I was deaf because I was able to speak well. Sometimes my friends would whisper in my ears and I would turn around and say to them, "My ears can't lipread."

While driving up a hill on Ames Street I realized, Don must have been drunk.

"Watch this," he said accelerating up to 70 mph up the hill. I yelled at him to stop the car. He was at the peak of the hill and there was an oncoming car driving by. Don panicked, swerved, and crashed into the next oncoming car.

It was a mess and it was a good thing he had a big car, and no one was seriously hurt. I looked at Don. "You're stupid!" I said and walked out of the car with no cuts or bruises.

On my way home I kept thinking that this is a life I didn't want, but everywhere I went, something bad seemed liked it was about to happen.

Finally, back at my apartment and my temporary roommate was drinking. He wanted me to join him in going out and driving around.

"No way! I just got back from an accident and he was drinking!"

I didn't like joining my friends driving around doing nothing anyway. Besides that, it was hard to lipread all the guys in the car.

My roommate went out with his friends that night and I went to a Boston Bruins game with my cousin Danny. A few days later, I read in the newspaper, two of my friends out the four got killed in a car crash that night crashing into a tree at 100 mph. My roommate fortunately survived but with many broken bones.

The Fire Alarm

One day after school, I met up with some of my friends at a social club called the British Club. A good friend I grew up with, Paul, teamed up with me playing a card game called 45. After winning the first round we walked over to the bar, ordered a drink, and watched the Boston Bruins. I got up from the barstool and headed to the men's room to wash my hands. When I walked out of the bathroom, I saw that everybody was gone.

"Okay, guys, you can stop playing games on me!" I yelled.

I walked to the bar but no one was behind it. The Bruins game was still on, so I sat down and watched. A few minutes later all the guys started coming back into the building. They were stunned that I was still inside.

"There was a fire alarm," one if my friends said. "We forgot you were deaf!"

Adventures in Deaf-land

One afternoon I joined my friend Billy in making sure no one stole his prized Ford Mustang from an open lot at a repair shop after hours. We got to the lot and his car was there, but the keys were inside the garage, which was closed.

"I know how to pop the trunk," he said. "I can crawl in and disconnect the wires. That way, no one can steal it."

We got out of my car and went over to the Mustang. Billy jiggled the lock on the trunk and got it open. He crawled inside. I laughed watching him crawl through his own car. He crawled to the front seat of the car, sat in the driver's seat, and unplugged the ignition.

He was just getting out, ready to shut the door, when I saw a black car approaching, lights flashing on the grill and the dashboard. A man got out of the black car quickly and approached Billy and me.

Billy told the man it was his car but the man didn't believe him. He started talking to me, but it was dark, and I couldn't lipread him. So, I told him that I was deaf.

Billy told me later the man had shouted, "Don't mess with me! I'll press more charges against you!"

Two policemen arrived in another car.

Billy started laughing. He told the first man, who turned out to be a detective, that I really was deaf. The man pushed Billy and me into the back seat of his car and made us put our hands on top of the front seat so that we could be handcuffed.

"I can't believe he doesn't believe you're deaf," Billy said while laughing

I started laughing, too. "I'm going to jail because I'm deaf."

I could lipread one of the detectives telling me to shut up. But Billy and I couldn't stop laughing. They asked Billy for proof for that it was his car. He didn't have his registration with him. They called his parents for verification.

After being convinced that the car belonged to Billy, one of the detectives asked Billy's mother if I was deaf.

"Oh," he said after a long pause.

Billy started laughing again. The officers and the detective didn't seem to like us, but they uncuffed us. "What do you expect a deaf guy to look like?" I asked one of them. "Just because I could speak, doesn't make me hearing."

Being deaf, you run into a lot of surprises, both good and bad. People would give me attitude, believing that I was ignoring them when I couldn't hear them.

One time, I walked alone into a deli in Lawrence. I got up to the counter to order a hot sub. Apparently there was a guy behind me yelling at me, and of course, I had no idea. I looked on at the vendor who had fear in his eyes.

"Are you okay?" I asked

He said nothing, but the guy behind me grabbed and pushed me into the table.

"What the heck going on?" I yelled.

The woman next to me knew I was deaf. "The idiot was screaming behind you to get out of his way," she said.

"I guess he was too stupid to figure out I was deaf."

We both laughed. The owner was too chicken to throw him out and the sweet lady calmed me down from going after the guy. She treated me to a nearby restaurant. Being deaf had its ups and downs but it always encouraged me when I met someone who had a good heart.

Falling in a Swamp

With everything going on during college, I had almost forgotten I was going blind. I spent a lot of weekends going to the beach in Salisbury. There was an amusement park there called The Center and you could see the wooden roller coaster from a mile away in 1979. We arrived at 8 p.m. on a cool evening at the end of July. Billy was driving my 1968 green Mustang. Another friend, Mark, was in the front seat, and I was in the back.

When we got to Salisbury Beach we passed a swamp and Billy took a left turn just before The Center. We parked a walking distance from the Center and Billy gave me my keys. I told him I would meet him in half an hour in front of Tripoli's Pizza, my favorite pizza restaurant. I was exhausted and wanted to nap. I fell asleep for more than a half hour.

Billy and Mark decided to come back to the car but they couldn't open the door, and I wouldn't wake up. So, they went back to the park.

I woke up when it was dark and realized that I was late. I hurried out of the car. But I couldn't see well in the dark, because of my night blindness. I wasn't able to make out how close the swamp was and I fell in. It was up to my neck and the flies wouldn't stop attacking me. I tried grabbing for dry ground but it was like trying to get out of quicksand.

Eventually, I got out but it felt like I had fallen into a septic tank. I was wet and muddy. I wanted to go home and shower, but I had to find Billy and Mark first. I walked into The Center looking as if I had just crawled out of the grave. People looked at me as if they were scared. *That's right*, I thought, *I'm a zombie!*

I finally found Billy and Mark who were both walking around looking for me. They had checked the car again, and I wasn't there. "I can't see in the dark. Why did you leave me there?"

I realized my night blindness was becoming noticeable, but it wasn't going to stop me.

Flying a Cessna

Summer of 1980 was eventful for me. I wanted to do everything I could; I loved adventure.

I was driving with a friend named Ken, and we were passing by the Lawrence airport.

"Let's fly a plane," I said to Ken

"Are you crazy?" he asked.

"Yeah!" I turned into the Lawrence Airport and parked my car. We walked inside the lobby "Let's go outside and see if we can find someone who owns a plane."

We walked around, I saw a guy near a Cessna, and asked him if it was his plane. It was and he asked me if I wanted to go for a ride.

"Yes!" I said. "Can I fly the plane, too?"

He agreed but Ken didn't want to join us.

"You're just a chicken," I teased him.

"I hope you come back in one piece," Ken said causing the guy to laugh hard.

"My name is Woody, and this is my chicken friend, Ken."

The guy laughed again. "My name is Frank. Nice to meet you both."

I got into the pilot seat and Frank showed me the gauges and gave me some basic instructions about flying. I was lipreading him, and I felt I had to let him know that I was deaf.

It's no big deal," Frank said.

We taxied to the runway. Frank was showing me what to do, and of course he was assisting. We took off just below the clouds.

The view of Lawrence and the Merrimack River was stunning. "Are we actually seeing the mountains in Vermont and New Hampshire?" I asked Frank.

"Oh, yeah," he replied. "It doesn't seem that far? Steer to 10 o'clock." I made a big turn, and he pointed. "There's Boston, there."

The sun was shining off the skyscrapers and it was absolutely gorgeous. Suddenly, the engine started sputtering. That got Frank's attention quickly, but soon then the engine returned to normal.

"Do you want to head back?" Frank asked. "The engine doesn't sound too good."

"No, we'll be fine," I said. "If it stalls, we could glide into the river."

He chuckled. "I can see why your friend thinks you're crazy!"

I laughed and continued flying around the city of Lawrence, looking at the sights and following the Merrimack River.

Soon Frank signaled that it was time to go back. After he landed the plane, I thanked him and handed him some cash.

Ken was in awe and a bit jealous after I told him how incredible it was up in the sky. I felt great and being deaf and going blind was the last thing on my mind. I was accomplishing things yet my friend who could see and hear perfectly was afraid. That made me feel good.

The Swim to the Lobster Buoy

During late summer some friends and family and I were staying in a cottage in Salisbury Beach. One night we had a bonfire and cookout, and a lot of friends came over.

There was a lobster buoy way out in the water. My friend Paul said he'd pay me $50 if I swam to the buoy. It was getting dark and I wasn't even thinking about my night blindness—I was competitive and I wanted to stun everyone!

With at least twenty people watching and thinking that I wouldn't dare go that far out, I jumped in the water and started swimming. The current helped more than I had expected. I got to the lobster buoy and was holding onto it. But it had gotten even darker. I couldn't see anyone at the beach, and they couldn't see me; I was too far out.

I was holding the buoy, resting, and trying to figure out which direction would take me back. Then I saw the bonfire, and I knew I was okay.

Suddenly, something touched my shoulder. It was a lifeguard and then another. The two of them pulled me out of the water and into their boat. One of them had a flashlight and pointed it on himself. "You could have easily been swept out by the current," he said.

They took me back to shore. Everyone on the beach was upset. "We thought you drowned! We called the lifeguards." They all gave me a hug and told me never to do that again.

But I brushed it off. "Aren't you forgetting something?" I asked. "Where's my fifty bucks?"

My eventful summer ended with so much joy. but getting back to reality was harder.

The two years since high school had been unsteady, and I still felt directionless. Luckily the community college I was attending was my safe haven. The support office was definitely my favorite hangout. There were a lot of students who would socialize in the office or nearby. Near the office was a large lounge and every Friday afternoon, there was a movie, and sometimes it would have subtitles.

One Friday afternoon after watching *Young Frankenstein* with everyone, Ruben waved me over. "I've got some good news," he said. "I've got an application from Gallaudet College for you."

"What's Gallaudet?" I asked.

He sat me down in his office and explained that it's a college for the deaf in Washington, D.C.

I sure liked hearing "Washington, D.C.," but I didn't know sign language. Ruben said that I could learn sign language there during the month before school started.

I thought it sounded good, but I didn't think I could pass their test, because I couldn't even understand the professors at my community college. It made me feel stupid.

"You're smarter than you think you are," he said with an encouraging smile.

I took the test, and Ruben mailed it to Gallaudet College. I honestly didn't think I would hear from them.

Three months later in mid-March I went to see Ruben after class to see if anyone was hanging out in the support office. I walked in and a few people were there. "Woody," he said waving me over. "I've got some great news for you. You passed your test to get into Gallaudet."

"Really?" I was surprised. I had put it out of my mind.

"You should go," he said. "It would be great for you. Sign the papers, and we'll get you ready."

A couple of my friends were pushing me to go as well. I got to thinking I was pretty much done with Massachusetts, and going to Washington, D.C. would be another dream come true.

"Sure," I said. "I'm going for it." I was looking for an escape from all the craziness and turmoil I was going through. For the past few years I felt like I had a death wish and I had quite a few friends killed in car crashes and at this point I didn't want to be the next one to die. I needed to settle down, but would Washington help me do that?

On my last day at the community college, Rubin and my friends had a little farewell party for me. I was grateful for them. They were a little slice of normal during my years right after high school.

When summer came along, me and five friends went to a concert at the Boston Garden to see Cheap Trick. When we got to the Garden, my friends all got drunk and high. The concert was wild, of course, and there was no way I would let any of my friends drive so I took my friend's keys and said, "I'm sober and I'm driving!"

It was safer for a guy who was deaf and had night blindness to drive. I couldn't wait to get out of Massachusetts and away from all the madness in my life.

My parents had a big goodbye party for me. Later that summer All my relatives were there celebrating my departure. My mother handed me a check from the fundraisers that was to be divided among my two sisters and me. It was the money that was left after our three trips to Russia. I was able to use the funds for books and supplies for school.

I was living at my friend's house and had the plane ticket to Washington hidden in a German mug on a shelf above the window in the living room. The night before leaving I finally took out the ticket. I went to bed early because my parents were going to pick me up and take me to Logan Airport.

I fell asleep quickly but had a terrible nightmare and screamed. I had actually dreamed that I was being stabbed. It felt completely real. I got that same nightmare every once in a while. I hoped that going to D.C. would put an end to the nightmares and my days of being out of control.

CHAPTER FOURTEEN

GALLAUDET

Gallaudet College (now called Gallaudet University) is a college for the deaf and the hard of hearing. It's the only liberal arts college in the world for the deaf. All professors and staff are required to know sign language to communicate with the deaf and hard of hearing students.

I arrived at Washington National Airport at noon on a gorgeous but swelteringly hot day. After getting off the plane, I raced to the baggage claim, picked up my bags, and went out to the front of the airport. I felt free like I did when I went off by myself in Moscow. I could see many cabs lined up and trains on the bridge nearby. I approached a cab driver and asked if he could take me to Gallaudet College on Florida Avenue.

"Sure kid. Get in," he said and then put my bags in the trunk.

I was thrilled to see what Washington would be like. The cab driver drove near the Washington Monument and then the Capitol, which was bright white with charming flowerbeds everywhere.

When we arrived at Gallaudet, I was surprised to see that it looked like a fort, with a security station inside the gate. The guard asked me if I was there for the summer orientation program using his voice and signing. I said I was and he gave the cab driver directions. We drove past the football field and then to Benson Hall, an eight-story building where a sign by the door read SVP Orientation.

When I went into the lobby with my bags, I saw a table and two staff members who waved me over. I signed next to my printed name and was given my room number and key.

I walked to the elevator, struggling with my bags. A young lady who was hard of hearing approached and offered to help. We got to the fourth floor and we brought my bags to the room.

I thanked her, but she insisted on showing me around, telling me where her room was.

Is she flirting with me? I wondered. I told her that I was amazed how clean and nice the dorm was.

She smiled. "Meet me in the lobby and we can get together for dinner tonight."

Is she asking me out already? I thought.

I went back into the room to unpack. I was hoping I would not get a roommate and I would have a big room all to myself. Eventually I went to the lobby to explore and meet new people. I saw many people signing, but there were a few who knew just a little sign language. I felt awkward, like I was in Moscow all over again trying to figure out what people were saying.

A girl came over to me and asked for my name. I didn't know if she would understand me, but she was able to lipread me well. Clearly, I wasn't used to meeting other deaf or hard-of-hearing people. One hearing guy, an interpreter, introduced me to everyone, and I felt relieved. It helped me get acquainted. I was comfortable with the hard-of-hearing people because I didn't know sign language, and the hard of hearing people understood what I was saying. One of the deaf guys had amazing lipreading skills. He thought I was hard of hearing at first and was surprised to find out that I was totally deaf.

I had to adjust to a few things when I first got to Gallaudet. I wasn't so sure I made the right decision going to a college visually impaired and also being deaf—and without knowing sign language. I felt awkward watching people sign. The common questions everyone asked me were, "What's your name?" "Where are you from?" "Are you hard of hearing?" Going in the cafeteria was different for me, deaf people were signing everywhere, and I felt a bit uneasy. But at least I had the girl who helped me to my room at my side that first day.

The orientation was a four-week program for new students who knew little or no sign language, so I wasn't totally lost. I met nice people and was excited by some of the activities.

In sign language class, we were given a sign name. The first letter of your name had to be used to identify your personality or identity. My sign name was "Lucky Woody." Many friends called me "Lucky" back in Massachusetts when I survived the many risks I took or certain near-death situations.

There were lots of adventures and a lot of sign language training. We took trips to Baltimore's Inner Harbor, Ocean City, Hershey Park, Kings Dominion, and tours all over Washington. After a few weeks into the program, I thought that going to Washington was the best decision I had ever made. There were many hearing women studying sign language at the college over the summer. I took a few out on dates to Georgetown for dinner or toured the museums. Going to Gallaudet College started to feel like a vacation.

I learned a little more sign language during the orientation and started my first year at Gallaudet. It took time to master sign language but the fact that everyone on campus was signing helped greatly. Oddly enough, American Sign language (ASL) started confusing my English. I was puzzled trying to figure out what people signing in ASL were saying at times. The words were scrambled. I was too used to speaking in English. Those who signed in ASL had a hard time understanding my signing, which was structured in proper English sentences. I actually learned two languages while in college, ASL and Russian.

Early on in the semester I joined a bowling team and worked as a layout editor for the school's newspaper, *The Buff and Blue.* I started making a lot of friends, especially through sports. I played recreational baseball and had night games under the lights. I kept my eye disease a secret until I was running to home plate and didn't see the catcher near me and knocked him over. A fight was about to happen. I apologized and told him I had tunnel vision and apparently the guy understood and hugged me. I was shocked because if this was my high school, it would have been a brawl. I soon learned to let people know I was visually impaired to prevent conflicts.

I had to learn to adjust to the deaf culture. I did well in courses that had teachers that signed in proper English. Some of the hard of hearing were also advantaged by hearing teachers using their voice and signing.

My dorm room was on the fourth floor and I roomed with a hard of hearing guy who loved sports cars. Unfortunately, at the start of my first semester I was having terrible nightmares. It got so bad that I had to visit the hospital to figure out what was going on. The doctors couldn't figure it out, even though I woke up from a nightmare in the middle of the night at the hospital. At least I was going to a deaf college where no one would hear me when I woke up.

On my first fall break, I took Amtrak from Union Station in D.C. to Boston. I saw a group of deaf people from Gallaudet on the train. One guy, Peter, introduced himself and we ended up having a long, interesting conversation.

Coincidentally, after the break, I had an eye appointment at the campus infirmary.

"There's a student who lives in Carlin Hall, on the fifth floor," the nurse said. "He also has Usher syndrome. His name is Peter."

Is this the guy I met on the train? I wondered

Right after the appointment, I went to Carlin Hall to see if I could find Peter. His name was on one of the doors on the fifth floor. I pressed the doorbell, which operated a strobe light. It was Peter who opened the door; the same guy I had met on the train. When I told him about my Usher syndrome, we immediately connected and found out we had a lot in common. We ended up being roommates and fast friends. Peter was an outgoing guy but I was the wild one. I invited him to join me to many events and we always had fun without thinking about our eye problems.

Washington Plane Crash

In January of 1982, spring semester began. A couple of people asked me if I wanted to go shopping in Georgetown. I took the opportunity. There was a big snowstorm that day; around 18 inches of snow fell as we headed to Georgetown. While we were stopped at a light, I saw a plane very close to hitting some buildings. The plane was turning and descending toward the river.

I jumped out of the car, screaming, "That plane is going to crash!"

My friends thought I was crazy and were yelling at me to get back in the car.

"I'm sure that plane crashed," I said. "I saw it!"

They didn't believe me. In my mind, I was imagining how scary it would be to be on that plane ready to crash.

We drove on through the heavy snow for a few blocks, and then we got stuck in the snow. I got out of the car to push. As we were pushing, an electrical shock ran through my body. Every time I moved, *zap!* The snow was heavy and wet and there was snow in my boots. About five feet from me was a streetlight that must have been turned on prior to my getting shocked.

It was 4 p.m. and getting dark. My friend Tom and his girlfriend, Teresa, were freaking out and didn't know what to do. Every time I moved I got a big shock.

Tom ran to a nearby building and knocked on the door hard. An elderly man answered, and Tom told him that I was getting shocked every time I moved.

I was freaking out. My whole body was buzzing, and whenever I moved there was a big buzzing!

The elderly man made a quick phone call to the authorities. They shut off the street lights, and I was free. "I thought I was going to die," I said.

Tom patted me on the back and laughed. "Let's get something to eat." We went to Uno's in Georgetown, which was one of my favorite restaurants, and then we headed back to Gallaudet. I went into the dorm, and there were a bunch of people watching the news. Air Florida Flight 90 had crashed into the 14th Street Bridge and into the Potomac River. We later found out that seventy-four of the seventy-nine people on board died, and years later the crash was the subject of several made-for-TV movies.

"I told you I saw it crash!" They were stunned.

In one day, I saw a snowstorm, I saw a plane crash, and I was shocked by a faulty street light.

The Moustache

Working for the David Taylor Naval Base in Annapolis, Maryland was a great job to have while in college. You could see all the ships come through the bay while sitting on the dock during lunch break. I loved watching the navy ships. I became fascinated reading the names of each passing ship. Across from the bay was the Naval Academy. I took a walk there during one lunch break, and there were people there making the movie *The Right Stuff*.

My boss was a friendly, sociable guy. He gave me work that was not part of my computer science major. He specialized in X–raying the metal of the ship's hull. My job was to collect all the data from the research files on the computer. My boss took me out for lunch and tried to have a conversation with me.

"You're hard to lipread because your moustache is so overgrown," I told him.

He chuckled. The next morning, he came to work, and his moustache was well trimmed. "Can you read my lips now, Woody?" he asked looking directly at me.

"You didn't have to trim it that short," I said with a laugh.

"What did your wife think of it?" a co-worker asked him.

"She was upset with me this morning," my boss said with a big grin.

"Tell your wife you did it for a good cause," I said with a wink.

Skydiving

I saw a flyer in the Gallaudet student lounge that got my attention: SKY-DIVING it said. I was excited. All transportation was provided. You just had to sign up and make the payment.

I signed up and told my friends about it. Four other people came along with me. The campus van took us to Ridgley, Maryland. Once we arrived, there would be six hours of training. An interpreter for the deaf was provided. We learned the safety procedures for skydiving and what to do in case the chute didn't open up properly. The instructor, Bob, was a lot of fun.

There was a deaf girl in our group who was a bit frustrated through the training. In training, they hang you on ropes from the ceiling and you have to pull the toggle on your shoulder.

She kept saying, "I can't!"

"We have a rule here," Bob said. "No one says, 'I can't.' Do you get it, miss?"

She agreed with a whimper and everybody completed their training. There was enough time to go on the plane and jump. We all strapped on our chutes, Bob made sure everyone was strapped in properly, and we put on our helmets.

I couldn't wait. The interpreter, Allison, seemed to be the only other person who was happy to be there. The two other hearing guys were just quiet. The other group of hearing-impaired people would be taking the next flight.

The five of us got into the plane with Bob and took off. When we reached 7,000 feet, Bob opened the door and you could feel the pressure. He threw a red flag out the door to check where it would land as well as the direction of the wind while the plane circled.

"We're good," the pilot said.

Bob looked at us. He picked the "I can't" girl first. I was watching, sure I would win my bet. The girl got up as Bob grabbed her safety cord and attached it to the floor.

"You ready?" Bob asked.

She looked out the door and backed off immediately. "I can't!"

"Come on, you can do it!"

"I can't! I can't!" she said with tears running down her face.

"Free jump for me!" I said to Bob.

He laughed and called one of the other guys to come forward. He showed him the procedure and said, "Jump!"

The guy jumped. Bob then called me over. I tried to lipread every instruction. "Put your feet on the plate above the wheel. Put your hands on the wing's rail."

I looked down for the first time sky diving. It felt as though I was jumping to my death. I looked at Bob. "Feet off the platform and hold the rail till I say go."

I nodded.

"Go!"

I let go of the rail, and the strap pulled the chute open. Finally, I was gliding to earth. I looked up to make sure my chute was fine and not a Mae West, meaning in the shape of a bra. In that case, you have to release that chute and pull the secondary. Thank goodness I didn't get a Mae West. Second thing I had to make sure of was that the sun was at 3 o'clock, on my right, so that way I would be going toward my target.

I looked down, and everything was tiny. When the wind blows, you can feel the sway.

As I got closer to the ground, I saw where I was, the bullseye on the field. I was about to land. I had to look at the horizon, because looking at the ground tricks your eyes. Then I used the toggle brakes on the chute for a softer landing. As I landed, I rolled sideways to avoid a hard impact that can cause an injury. I actually landed well.

I got up, wondering where the other people who jumped before me were. The owner of the skydiving club approached me. "You did great! The other people landed in the trees. You may be deaf, but the other guys have handicapped brains!"

I laughed, and he gave me a high five. Then I saw Bob land. "Great jump," he said and then asked me if I was ready to jump again.

"Yes," I said. "I want to free jump!"

The Washington Capitals

I met a hard-of-hearing guy named Keith. He loved ice skating and hockey. I would go to Fairfax, Virginia to go ice skating at a public rink every Friday with him. Outside the skating rink, there was a beautiful view of the Capitol, lit up at night. Keith and I were hoping to come up with the Gallaudet hockey team.

Keith and I met a cool hockey coach. He named our team the Washington Silent Capitals. It was hard finding players, but the coach had everything planned out. Keith told me that we had a game the following Saturday night. We would be playing in Fairfax, Virginia.

I was excited. I didn't even bother to ask who we were playing against. I was so enthusiastic.

The coach got us prepared during the week. "I hope I can play well with my tunnel vision," I said to Coach.

"I've seen you play," Coach said. "It's no problem."

On game day, we all gathered to get on the bus. We were excited about playing our first game. We got to Fairfax Ice Arena and into the locker room, and I realized that there were only ten or twelve of us. A few guys I barely recognized were on our team. We put on our skates and then I shook the hands of the new guys. We were all given Washington Capitals team shirts because we were the Washington Silent Capitals. I was concerned that I wouldn't be able to see enough to play. I didn't want us to end up looking like the Washington Blind Capitals.

We got on the ice and started skating around and shooting the pucks to warm up the goalie. It felt good to be playing ice hockey again, but I was rusty. I felt like a blind man on ice. I was stressing myself to see where the puck was. Looking for the puck was like playing hockey with binoculars.

When the game was about to begin, I asked the coach, "Why are there a lot of people in the stands? Are they curious how deaf people play hockey?"

"Get on the ice, Woody!" Coach said with a laugh.

The game started. I was hoping the referee knew that I couldn't hear the whistle. *The other two guys are hard of hearing*, I thought, *but they can probably hear the whistle. Well, I'll find out.*

The game played on. The opposing team shot the puck to the end of the rink. I skated as hard as I could, and when I got to the puck, I looked up. Everybody was still on the other side of the rink. I looked over to the coach and he was laughing. I realized that the referee had already blown the whistle. When I raced down the entire rink, I couldn't see to my sides, so I didn't know if I was being followed. I got to be the first Blind Capital.

While the game was being played, I got knocked down. When I went back on the bench, I found my way to Coach. "Geez, these guys are really good! Who the heck are they? They look like professionals."

"They're the Washington Capitals. This is a charity game."

I had no idea that some of my teammates were former Capitals. I couldn't believe it. I got back to the locker room, and my friend Keith pulled me aside. "Do you know who you're sitting next to? He was one of the top scorers in the National Hockey League last year."

"He doesn't look like Wayne Gretzky or Mike Bossy."

The Capitals player laughed. He was Dennis Maruk—I think. Back in those days, when I got introduced to people, I could never lipread their names. I didn't bother asking my friend to repeat the name. I would have paid more attention if he'd been a Boston Bruins player. I admired my friend Keith for putting an effort to make this hockey game happen.

It was hard getting serious in college, but sign language made college a little easier at times. It depended on who the teacher was. Liberal arts classes were easy, but my major was in computer science, and some of the professors from Maryland University could not sign well. It made a lot of things difficult. I wanted to understand the course and not just assume I understood.

At times during my holiday breaks, I would fly on my favorite airline, People Express. Once I took a flight from Boston to Washington. I went up to the door of the cockpit, which was open.

"What's up?" the copilot asked.

"Oh, I was just wondering what it was like in the cockpit." I then I asked him if I could talk to the people on the microphone and he said okay. He turned on the microphone. "Ladies and gentlemen, you have a deaf pilot flying the plane!"

The pilots were laughing. I gave him back the microphone, said thanks, and walked back up the aisle. People were laughing and some were clapping. I waved and sat in my seat. The person who sitting next to me patted me on the back. "You should have seen some of the faces of the people before they realized you were joking," he said.

In the summer of 1983, I worked at Naval Air Station Patuxent River, in Maryland. I enjoyed working there. I programmed, tested, and designed sonar buoys for tracking submarines. Every morning, we had to listen to the Star Spangled Banner and salute. I lived in the barracks on the base over the summer. Every morning at 6 a.m. you would hear or feel all the fighter jets fly by the barracks and shake the place. You didn't need to be able to hear to wake up in the morning. The jets would shake you out of your bed. On weekends, I would take a bus to Washington and spend the time going out with the summer students.

Working for the Navy was an adventure. They even had their own air show every summer. I loved their air shows and wished I could fly those planes.

The Air and Space Museum

One thing I loved about Gallaudet College was that they had a good summer co-op program that enabled deaf people to gain work experience in their field. My summer jobs had nothing to do with computer science, but I enjoyed working for the Navy doing interesting computer and hands-on work.

I spent a lot of time with the graduate and summer students from Gallaudet. We would go to happy-hour every Friday by the Potomac River and go on paddle boats at night on the Fourth of July to watch the fireworks from the Jefferson Memorial. It was a great view. We would all gather together at a picnic area and practice our signs; there was always a great social gathering.

We would go touring around Washington on weekends. One time we went to the Air and Space Museum, my favorite museum. One of my favorite things there was the "SS Pussywillow," by Rowland Emett. It was a gorgeous abstract design of a pussywillow tree that looked like a spacecraft. I used to visit the SS Pussywillow so often that, at some point, it made me feel like I could hear the movements and sounds coming from the spacecraft with all the spinning objects. I had the sounds orchestra in my ears of the SS Pussywillow for so many years.

One time, after spending a couple of hours in the museum, we all walked out of the building and sat on the steps, watching people and talking. A guy behind me was saying something. A lady in front of me gestured to indicate that someone behind me was talking to me. I turned around. "I'm deaf, but I can lipread well," I said. "Can you please repeat what you were saying?"

The guy was scared. He jumped away, screamed, and ran through the crowd. All my friends were laughing. "Make a note of it," I said. "Deaf people can be hazardous to strangers, people!"

Washington DC was fun during holidays and was always a good time to be around, especially the Christmas tree lightings. In 1983, I took my date to see the Lawrence Welk show there and President Ronald Reagan showed up. It was such a beautiful evening, with a few snowflakes, like a dream. I only wished I could hear the Lawrence Welk orchestra at that time but seeing all this was a dream come true.

I had a part time job at the National Governor's Association. Every office represented a state, and each had a cubicle in front of the office for the secretary. I was an assistant to all the secretaries, delivering mail, documents, etc. Many of the secretaries whined so much that their assistants would quit. My boss was always having fun with me, because I wasn't complaining about anything going on with the secretaries. I couldn't hear all the nonsense. I just did my job.

My boss took me out for lunch a few times and was amazed that I could lipread much of what went on with the secretaries. It was a political soap opera, but I had a great time working there. On my last day, my boss and co-workers treated me to lunch and gave me an Appreciation Award.

I loved Gallaudet College for many reasons—the summer jobs, the society, the activities, and some of the education. It was an overall good educational experience. I felt I had to go to Gallaudet College not to just learn sign language, Pascal, or Russian but to do something constructive, adventurous, and do something that would use my brain.

I applied to Rochester Institute of Technology and got accepted there. I had decided what I really wanted to do.

I had a great time exploring Washington D.C., though. I will always cherish the memory of those days. On my final day, I was all packed and ready to travel to New Jersey and then to Rochester, New York.

The Phone Booth

I left D.C. and flew to Newark, New Jersey. When I got off the plane and walked to the baggage claim, the place was like a bunch of ants fighting for food. I picked up my bags and looked for the woman who was supposed to pick me up. I soon learned she was a procrastinator. Fifteen minutes passed, and nothing.

I hated to be in a situation like that, because when you're deaf, you have to find someone to interpret for you when you make a phone call. I started asking people, but they kept passing me as if I was invisible. I saw a cop, so I approached him, told him I was deaf, and asked if he would make a phone call for me. He said he was too busy and couldn't.

If I grabbed his gun out of his holster, would he be too busy to try to get it back? I thought. I was frustrated. I walked through the crowd to the phone booth, hoping for a miracle. I put the quarter in the slot. I dialed the number, waited a few seconds, then said, "This is Woody. I'm at the airport lobby waiting for you." I hung up. The quarter came back out. I was frustrated. I assumed the number was busy.

I looked behind me. Two men were impatiently waiting for the phone. I tried again—re-dialed the number, assumed two rings, then spoke. "This is Woody. I'm at the airport lobby waiting for you." I hung up, and once again, the quarter came out.

I looked behind me. Now there were three guys waiting.

The man behind me yelled at me. "What are you doing?"

I told him, "I'm deaf, and I needed to make a phone call for a friend of mine to pick me up." I asked the guy if he would help.

"Sure," he replied.

I put the quarter in the slot, dialed the number, and gave the phone to the guy. It looked like somebody answered. He relayed my message, hung up the phone, and told me that she was on the way. Bingo!

I was relieved and thanked him. I picked up my bags, started walking, and there she was, the procrastinator.

CHAPTER FIFTEEN

COLLEGE LIFE

I started at Rochester Institute of Technology (RIT) in 1985 with the intended major industrial design. This time, I did not have to learn sign language—or any language, for that matter.

I had an interpreter in all of my classes who signed in English language clearly. I got along well with the interpreters at RIT—all women as luck would have it. Understanding the professors was not much of an issue. The only issue I would have was if the interpreter did not show up, which was awful and isolating but thankfully it didn't happen often. Learning all of the signs and understanding the deaf culture at Gallaudet got me prepared for RIT.

There were also a note taking service. I would ask someone in my class if anyone wanted to take notes for me and the support service would pay for their efforts. Note taking services were different in the 1980s than they are today, where someone is hired in advance to type every word the professor is saying with the ability to read the screen in real time while they are typing. I would have loved to have this technology when I was at RIT. I realize now how much information I missed back in the 80s. It was hard for someone like me, because I am deaf and functioning in the hearing world and cannot understand a hearing teacher, yet I cannot understand a deaf teacher who signs in ASL. I've always been the man in the middle.

It was hard to watch the interpreter at times when listening to a lengthy lecture. I would fall asleep like the other students. The hearing students had better advantage and were able to put their head down to listen to the lecture. I could not do that.

Reeling in New Friends with a "Fish"

I once lived in a dorm called Fish. I was doing a homework assignment on my desk, drawing and using black ink. My room door was wide open and some random guy came in. I got startled and spilled ink all over my project.

"My name's Scott," he said while laughing and helped me clean up the mess.

"I'm Woody. Not nice to meet you," I said and we both laughed.

He was asking me a question and as I turned around he realized I was deaf. He tapped on my shoulder and said, "I am amazed that you can lipread and speak well!" Me, Scott, and his roommate Mike have all been great friends ever since.

The Diner

Later that year we all went to a diner. When the waitress took our orders, I ordered a hamburger. She asked if I wanted fries, but she was holding her order pad over her mouth, and I could not read her lips. She realized I did not understand the question. She assumed I was a foreign and asked Mike, "How do you say, 'French fries' in his language?"

"You can say it in any language you want," Mike said. "He is still not going to hear you. He's deaf." Scott and Mike were laughing.

The waitress looked at me and said slowly and loudly, "DO YOU WANT SOME FRENCH FRIES?"

"Let's sit at another table," I said to Scott and Mike. "I'm not stupid," I said to the waitress, "talk to me normally, like everyone else."

Later in the meal Mike and Scott were teasing me putting their hands over their mouths so I could not understand what they were saying. All I could do was laugh.

I showed Mike and Scott some words that had the same lipreading patterns as other words. "Olive juice," I said only moving my lips while smiling at Scott. He was surprised and thought I said, "I love you." I laughed and explained that the two phrases are exactly the same in lipreading. "Olive juice" became popular.

It's Art?

While I was majoring in industrial design, I had to do a lot of drawings. In one class that I was in I had to draw a naked woman. Some students would offer to pose naked for these classes. A few women had asked me to pose for their photo shoot but no way I would do it, not me.

One time when I attended the class, a woman came up to me. "Hi, Woody, how are you?"

"Pretty well."

I was wondering what she was doing at the class. Then she walked onto the platform and took off her clothes, and I was drawing my friend's girlfriend. *How weird is this?* I thought. *I should make my friend jealous.*

After I finished the drawings, I walked out of class and into the corridor, and I saw the model's boyfriend. "Hey, do you want to see what I just drew?" I asked with a laugh.

"Sure."

I showed him my drawings. "It looks like my girlfriend."

"It is." His face turned red.

"Go to the door on your right," I said.

He had no idea his girlfriend was doing this, but that's art for you.

I spent my summer breaks with Scott's and Mike's families in Long Island. For one month, I stayed in Centereach where Mike lived, and then I stayed a month in Port Jefferson Station, where Scott lived. I got along well with both families. They generously took me out to many places. Mike was involved with the fire department in Centereach and there were so many outdoor activities, especially the cookouts, I loved the cookouts.

Mike's family took me to New York City a few times. Going to New York City for the first time was amazing. I could not take my eyes off all those skyscrapers. The buildings were in such perfect alignment with each other. I met Mike's Russian grandparents in Manhattan and later, Mike and I took off to the Empire State Building.

On the way back to Long Island, Mike's dad asked me what I thought of New York City.

"It's great, but it's nothing like Boston," I said with a smirk.

"We have taller buildings than you do!" he said with a laugh.

When we got back to the house, on the news, two guys jumped off the Empire State building with their parachutes and landed where cab drivers waited for them. I yelled at Mike, "Look what we just missed!"

When I met Scott's family in Port Jefferson, I grew close to his dad, Leon. We got along so well and he took me to many places and he would take me on his boat for a ride. We'd go spend a few hours having laughs, having drinks, and enjoying the sunset. I loved the boat so much and sometimes Scott would take me to Fire Island on the boat and we'd enjoy the beach.

During my years at RIT, I gained a lot of skills in product design and model-making. I loved making models of commercial products. I made many products for my portfolio, such as Dremel tools, flip phones, eyeglasses, and lobby chairs.

Having an interpreter throughout RIT was reliable. It made a big difference attending a hearing school with an interpreter.

I spent my summers in Long Island and worked for *Newsday*. I had to go from house to house trying to sell *Newsday* subscriptions. I came up with a touching, sordid story about my deafness to convince people I needed the money for college. My boss was impressed that I was able to do well as a deaf person. I hated it, though.

I also helped Scott's uncle Steve work at his TV repair shop in Queens. Just watching Steve drive was interesting. I should have videotaped him. I used to say to him, "I'm better off deaf when you drive!"

Scott also had a brother named Phil and I hung out with him at times. He was a singer and a professional musician. It was fun following him around. Phil knew many rock stars and introduced me to some famous ones in New York City. They thought it was cool that Phil had a deaf friend who could speak, even though they couldn't tell at first that I was deaf. I couldn't lipread all the big names I met, but I met some guys from Aerosmith and Kiss. They were pretty nice to me.

Phil was also a singer for Foghat for a short time. I first met Foghat at Penny Arcade in Rochester, New York. They gave me a pass and invited me on their bus after the concert. I was introduced to the whole band, and Phil and I caught up on things. Phil showed me around in the tour bus which was really cool. Later, while I was staying in Port Jefferson, Eric Cartwright and the rest of the band stayed for the weekend at the Port Jefferson house. We had barbecues and parties. I got to know all the guys.

"Do you want a deaf singer?" I asked Eric.

"Let's hear your voice," he said.

I paused. "I don't think so."

They laughed. They were cool, I enjoyed experiencing the tour bus and exploring the life of real rock stars.

After my third year at RIT, I noticed my vision had worsened and I was hoping not to lose my central vision because it was still relatively clear. I decided to get it checked at Massachusetts Eye and Ear in Boston. I was told I had cataracts and my visual fields was 20 degrees out of 180. Dr. Berson told me that I was legally blind, but my central vision was good.

I was twenty-eight-years old and I had never told anyone I was legally blind, but I did tell people I had tunnel and night vision loss. I was open about my eye problems, but I didn't believe I was legally blind and I have correctly proved that. After my cataract surgery two years later, my peripheral vision was 25 degrees. Therefore, I was not legally blind just yet, but it made me feel good that I didn't dwell on the results beforehand. I continued to drive and continued working on my goal, to be a designer. Looking at the medical papers was depressing and deceiving, but the reality was that I could see well enough and no one could predict when I was going totally blind.

"Maybe you should think about changing your major, Dr. Berson said. "You only have about ten years left in your vision"

"I refuse to believe that," I shouted.

"Just be careful in the things you do!"

No one could slow or weaken my resolve. I went to my car and drove straight to Bridgeport, Connecticut to take the ferry to Port Jefferson, Long Island. I stayed with Mike and Scott for the summer. Nobody could tell I was visually impaired and I was determined to continue my life without interruption. I felt the appointment at the eye doctor was deceiving because, as far as I was concerned, my eyes were working properly. I became more cautious when driving or doing things.

I graduated from Rochester Institute of Technology in 1989 and earned a bachelor's degree. When I picked up my diploma at graduation I was proud I had done something on my own.

CHAPTER SIXTEEN

THE DISCRIMINATORS

After I graduated from RIT, I started looking for a job in my field. I applied for several jobs in the Rochester area. I had a few interviews and wasn't super confident about how they went because my deafness turned out to be an issue.

I was interviewed at one company that does industrial and graphic design. When I met the interviewer, I told him that I was deaf and could lipread well. He rolled his eyes.

"Why are you giving me that look?"

"We had a deaf person before," he said impatiently. "We got rid of the guy."

"I'm not that guy," I said defiantly. "You have no right stigmatizing deaf people."

"We don't want to hire another deaf person."

I was tempted to punch him for such an insult. I walked out of the office and tried to stay calm and positive.

Okay, I told myself, *I'll just move on to the next interview.*

This time it was a big company that needed product designers. I was excited about this company. I loved product designing and the interviewer really liked my diverse background. He was impressed with my portfolio. I thought I was seconds away from landing the job but then he started to ask odd questions about deafness.

"What if there's a fire alarm?" he asked.

"You have many workers in the building. I'm sure I would notice when everyone gets up and leaves the building. Or someone could approach me to let me know. It's no big deal."

The interviewer was trying to think of another question, as if he were trying to make an excuse for not hiring a deaf person. "You won't be able to hear at meetings."

"Interpreters are provided, and I also can lipread. If you haven't noticed, you're interviewing me, and I'm understanding you well without an interpreter."

"We'll keep you in mind. Thank you for coming."

I knew what that meant. I must have had at least twenty interviews. I was astonished that most of the people interviewing me had no problem hiding their discriminatory attitudes.

I got discouraged. I had to look for something other than a professional job. I landed a third-shift job at Wegman's supermarket. I wasn't happy about it, but it was work.

While working at Wegman's, I ran into my friend Mike's old roommate, Paul. I became good friends with Paul, and we got an apartment in the very nice Park Avenue area. But I was desperate for a real job. Paul had landed a job right after college as an engineer which made me feel like a loser.

While we stayed at the apartment, I wanted to do some woodworking. I asked the landlord if I could put a table saw in the basement, which he agreed to. I bought a table saw and started doing some woodwork in the basement.

The people on the first floor weren't too happy with the noise. One guy came into the basement to tell me how loud the table saw was. He wanted to talk to me about a commercial building that had many vacant spaces for small businesses. He gave me some information about whom to contact. He was hoping I would give it a shot, and I liked the idea of working in a commercial building. I was even thinking; *Maybe I should start my own business. No more discrimination!*

I hated the third shift job at the supermarket, so I quit. I met with Tom, the owner of a building on East Main Street in Rochester. It was in a bad area, but I didn't care. I wanted to get somewhere in life. Tom showed me the 1,200 square foot space on the third floor. I loved it, it wasn't expensive to rent, and I took it. You could do anything you wanted with the space.

I loved woodworking, so I bought a few machines. I was also still looking for a real job. I ran into a guy in the parking lot of the business building. I saw him with a portfolio and thought he might be a designer. I asked him if he was.

"Yes. How did you know?"

"You're carrying a portfolio."

He laughed and asked, "Are you a designer, too?"

"Yes, and I'm looking for a full-time job."

"You've got yourself an interview," he said. "My name is Art. Come to my studio."

On my interview day, Art browsed through my portfolio and said, "You're hired."

I couldn't believe it. I had my own office in the heart of the city.

I also started a business designing and making birdhouses and bird-feeders. Between working for Art and working for myself I was getting quite busy. I started to sell my products at some local festivals.

It was thrilling to be able to create anything I wanted and sell it. I often stayed up all night in my wood shop to make products and at times made fifty birdhouses a day. I had created templates so it could be done more quickly. It was a lot of effort, but I was glad to be working.

Eventually, Art's business took a dive and it ran out of money. After a year, he laid me off. I wasn't too happy about it, but I had big thoughts about my own business. I decided to apply for a loan from the Small Business Administration (SBA). I had to have a business plan written and a good marketing plan set. I was approved, but the fees that came with the loan were astronomical. I bought all of the machines and tools to start doing business with retail stores.

The only thing I didn't like about the SBA was there was no working capital for the business. I had to hire a lawyer who ripped me off and there was no point in getting a loan when you had to pay all the fees to get it. The fees were 30% of my loan. I was hoping for a miracle that my business would take off.

The Buffalo Angel

On my free time on some weekends, I would go out a lot and when the Boston Bruins were playing the Buffalo Sabres, I would get tickets. Paul would pick me up at the business building, and we would head out to Buffalo. Once, we stopped by an Irish restaurant and bar a few hours before the game. It was a lot of fun, and of course the Buffalo fans were picking on me.

After dinner and drinks, we headed out to Buffalo Auditorium, which was in walking distance. We sat a bit high behind the net. Once we got there, some girls we had met in the bar were just behind us.

The Bruins lost in overtime and the place went wild. Paul and I headed back to the Irish bar to meet the ladies again. We stayed there for a few more hours. "It's almost 3 a.m.," Paul said. "Let's get going."

It was hard for me to leave all the fun people we were socializing with. We had to get back to Rochester and I had Paul drive, since it would be safer than a semi-blind man driving at night.

We were driving on I-90 through the city when a red light started blinking on the dashboard. Paul and I noticed it immediately. We decided to take the next exit.

"This is the Bronx of Buffalo." I warned Paul.

We got off the ramp and parked his Monte Carlo immediately. I opened the hood and saw the problem right away. I put my hand down by the fan and pulled out a fan belt! "Where are we going to find a fan belt at 3:00 in the morning?" I asked.

"We could walk down the road and see what's over there."

I figured if we left the car there it would have been stolen. Then I noticed that right across the street was a guy working on his van. "Hey, sir," I said while running across the street. "I need a fan belt. Do you know any gas stations around here?"

He didn't respond. Instead, he walked straight to the side of his van and got something out. Then we walked together to my car.

Paul was standing there by the car as if he were my security guard.

The guy installed a new fan belt in my car, tightened it, and shut the hood—just like that.

I freaked out and gave the guy a hug. "How much do you want?"

"Nothing. Don't worry about it."

"Really?"

"Really. Take care." And he left.

Paul and I got in the car. We were right back on the highway in less than ten minutes. We were both thinking that this guy had to have been an angel. It made me start to think if there really was a God out there watching over us.

TV Rolloff

Every week, I would go bowling at Olympic Bowl in Henrietta. I loved being in a league and in tournaments. Occasionally, I would try to qualify for a tournament with sixty-four other bowlers. The next step after that was to make the top four which would mean being on a Sunday morning TV Rolloff.

In 1990, I made the TV Rolloff for the big prizes twice, which was exciting because it meant I would be on TV. I won the first round. Because of my poor peripheral vision, when I got a strike, people would put their hands out for me to slap, but I wouldn't see it, making them think I was a conceited deaf guy. I told myself that it didn't matter because I got a strike on television.

One of the bowlers in the final round had a 200 average and yet I bowled a 237 and won the championship. I was introduced to the sportscaster of the local news, and the host of *TV Rolloff* announced the winner: Woody Livingston! I got up, and he called my girlfriend over as well. The host was overly dramatic and I could not understand what he was saying. He was trying to get my girlfriend to sign something but she couldn't follow him. Suddenly he turned the microphone toward me. I paused for a second. "It was my lucky day!" The host gave me a few prizes—free dinner, free drinks, free groceries—and then the plaque as the 1990–1991 champion, plus a nice check.

I might have been discriminated against by many people, but I could still find a way to keep the funds rolling in. And speaking of funds, I won the TV Rolloff again one month later, and I met the same overly dramatic host.

The Woodworking Business

I was trying to run a business as a totally deaf and visually impaired person, all by myself—and it wasn't easy. I hated sales, but I had to drive everywhere to make them. I went as far as Washington, D.C.

A store in Fairfax, Virginia was selling a lot of my birdhouses, but they wanted me to hand deliver them. I had a friend who worked at the National Institutes of Health in Maryland and it made the trip easier. I wanted to keep the business going until I could give up driving visually impaired for four hundred miles to deliver cedar birdhouses to make retail stores happy.

"I've been delivering birdhouses to you, and you've been selling quite a few, I'd like to ship the products to you for now on. I'm going blind and delivering birdhouses to you was taking too many risks."

"We don't want any more birdhouses from you."

I was stunned by their rejection.

I continued trying to make sales. When I succeeded, I had to race back to the shop to manufacture the birdhouses and feeders they ordered. I would say that I was discriminated against by more than half of the retail stores.

I went to one garden store that sold fifty of my birdfeeders. "You've now sold all the feeders that you bought from me. Are you ready to order some more?"

This woman couldn't have been nastier. "I don't like dealing with deaf people because I have to waste my time trying to talk to them."

"You sold all my products super fast."

"You're wasting my time."

Some retail stores were nice, but they were small, selling only a few birdhouses a month. I needed to get large orders. I tried looking for a marketing person and found this cool guy named Chuck. He was a good businessman and helped me get some things going. I hired salespeople, hoping they could make large sales. I went to trade shows in Columbus, Ohio and Syracuse, New York. I drained everything in my bank account to make the business work.

I hired high school kids, and they wouldn't listen to instructions. "Paint the wall and not the posts." When I checked on them, it was a disaster. There was paint all over the floor, paint all over the posts, and even paint on the ceiling. I wanted to pick up the gallon of paint and empty it over their heads. I had to tell them to go home.

At the end of one day, one of the sales guys came by. I was hoping for some large orders. I asked, "How many did you sell today?"

"Ten."

I was so disappointed. "That's it? What did you do all day?"

"I had an appointment, then I had to run some errands, and I stopped at two birdfeeder stores."

"You were supposed to stop at twenty stores," I replied. "When you want to make sales, you have to knock on all doors, not just a few. No wonder you got fired from your last sales job. It's because you're lazy."

I was at the end of my rope. I decided to make some phone calls using the relay service for the deaf.

The thing I hate about the relay service is the delay. It's a three–way conversation. You call the relay service using your telecommunication device for the deaf (TDD). You give them the number you want to call. The relay service dials the number and lets you know if it's ringing or if it's busy. When the person answers the phone, the relay explains the service to the person you're calling. Making a relay call having a three-way conversation is time consuming. I would say that 90% of the businesses I was working with did not want to deal with it. They would just hang up.

I had an important business call and I was using the relay service. I was having a conversation about a large order of birdfeeders, the biggest order yet. The relay service accidentally disconnected the person I was talking to.

I got nervous. I told the relay, "Hurry and call back!"

The store owner picked up the phone and said right away, "I don't want the deal anymore," and hung up.

Nothing was working out for the business. I came to a point where I said, "I'm tired of the discriminators." I decided to file bankruptcy and get out of the mess. I've always hated sales, and this was one of the reasons to hate it—encountering discriminators.

The Downfall

I moved my shop to the basement level in the building after bankruptcy. My friend Chuck had bought all the necessary machines from the Small Business Administration, so I was still able to do custom woodworking. I did it as a hobby and continued selling items at a few festivals in the area. But I had lost a lot of money. Eventually, I lost my truck, my machines, and my income, and I hit rock bottom.

For a time, I was homeless. I had to sneak into my business's building at night to stay warm. I slept in my wood shop. A few people came by occasionally and brought food. I was so lost. I had to find places to take showers at friends' houses and other places.

A woman spied on me. When I left the wood shop to go to the men's room, she snuck into my office and stole my credit card, check book, and business supplies. Then she left the building.

I walked inside the shop and shut off the lights, closed the door, and locked it. I stopped by the shop next door for a few minutes. Then I headed outside. Outside the building, there were cop cars and flashing lights. A cop came up to me. "Are you Woody Livingston?"

"Yes."

He said he had arrested a woman and asked if I knew her.

"She looks familiar. I saw her walking in the hallway yesterday."

"She stole all of this stuff of yours."

I was astonished. The bank teller from the bank across the street knew me well. He was there and greeted me by my name.

The cop continued, "The woman tried to cash your checks and use your credit card at the bank."

"For a few bucks?" I said with a laugh.

A few nights later, someone tried to steal my Honda Accord. I installed a secondary switch under the dashboard. They couldn't steal the car, but they stole all my bowling equipment from the trunk.

How much poorer could I get? The car had been given to me so that I could find a job.

Every Sunday, I would go over to the home of my friend Paul's family in Macedon. We would have a big dinner—spaghetti and meatballs and fresh French bread from Wegman's. Paul's family were all big Buffalo Bills fans. This was in the '90s when the Bills, with Jim Kelly, were popular and winning. They were so good that they were the only team ever to lose the Super Bowl four straight times.

I hated living in a business building. The discriminators had destroyed my hope for a job and my business. In fact, manufacturing birdfeeders is competitive and difficult no matter how great your design for the product are. Every time I designed a product, someone would steal my ideas. The only defense was being rich enough to patent the design. I was at the end of my rope, thinking, *What's the point of living?*

CHAPTER SEVENTEEN

THE TRUTH THAT SET YOU FREE

I was homeless for a few months and I started wondering, *Is there a God?* I started to ask some people in the business building. "When you die, where are you going?" I asked a few people. Some said, "Everything is done when you die. There's no heaven and no hell."

The answers bothered me. I thought there had to be a God. I was so curious and willing to know. I decided, "I'm going to pray and see what happens. If God answers my prayer, I'll believe in Him."

I knelt down. I prayed for the first time since I was a kid. I said, "God, I want a job and to settle down and have a family and a new life."

And that was it.

I got together with my friend Paul, and we went out to eat. After we ate, we sat at the bar to have a drink and watch sports. "Can you get the Red Sox on your TV?" I asked the bartender.

"My ex–husband was a big Red Sox fan," said a blonde woman sitting next to me.

"How about you?" I asked.

"I'm a Dodgers fan."

"We're going to get along just fine, because you're not a Yankees fan." She laughed, and we continued talking. I told her about the horrible downfall of my business.

"I'm a manager at the photo lab at Walmart," she said. "If you want to apply, I'll give you the job."

I was surprised and elated. I applied for the job at Walmart and was hired the following week.

I even took her out on a date as a thank you. I wasn't interested in someone who already had children. I wanted to marry a woman without kids, which is hard to find when you're in your early thirties. She was fine with that.

Working at the photo lab was difficult because of my tunnel vision. During rush hours, I would knock into things or bump into the other workers. The job required too much moving around for a deaf man with tunnel vision. I was able to do the job, but a bit more slowly than the other employees because I was being cautious.

I applied instead for a cashier's position, and I got that job a week later. Working as a cashier was pretty easy. I didn't have to listen to the customers bickering and complaining about everything. I would always tell the customers, "If you have a complaint, go to the manager. I'm deaf." It worked out well, at least for me.

During breaks, I would occasionally run into a woman named Jennifer. I tried talking to her, but she was hard to lipread. I put my hand on her shoulder so that she would look at me and I would be able to lipread her. She misinterpreted that and was offended. When I went back at the cash register, the supervisor wanted to see me. I met with the supervisor, and he said that Jennifer had filed a complaint against me for sexual harassment.

I started laughing. "I was trying to lipread her," I said. "I was just trying to get her attention."

The supervisor said it was all right, and I went back to the cashier station and back to work. A few days later, I started getting letters from Jennifer. She was asking me out, to go for a picnic or something. After I read that, I said to myself, "No way!" Jennifer wrote me a few more letters, and finally I decided I would give it a shot. "Okay, I'll pick you up tomorrow at your house."

She smiled. "Okay."

I went to Caledonia to pick Jennifer up and met practically her whole family. We got into my car and I drove to Letchworth State Park, where we picked out a spot for a picnic.

She was a bit hard to lipread, but I was able to communicate with her. While we were having the picnic, my mind was saying, "This is the woman you're going to marry." I was always afraid of making a commitment, but this was different. I was comfortable with her.

The next day, we went to the Avon Flea Market, where there were many arts and crafts vendors and a farmer's market.

While dating, the people at Jennifer's Bible study group were telling her that she should not be dating me because I was not a Christian. But Jennifer very much believed I was going to become a Christian.

Before she met me, she told everyone at the Bible study group that she had prayed for the name of the man she was going to marry, and God spoke to her the name Joseph Livingston.

Later, those people told me that they had heard my name two years before, but I laughed and said, "My name is Woodrow Livingston, so you've got it all wrong!"

Jennifer and I knew we were made for each other, and we didn't care what people thought when we decided to get married so soon after meeting each other.

One night, Jennifer's Bible study group was praying for me, and I woke up in the middle of the night with an amazing vision, as if I were flying through the universe having a tour with God. I realized that it was God getting my attention.

He certainly got my attention before I got married in December 1995, when I got mail from Massachusetts regarding my birth certificate. The birth certificate read Joseph Woodrow Livingston!

I called my birthplace in Massachusetts. They told me that my name was Joseph Woodrow Livingston.

"That can't be," I said in utter shock. "I have a birth certificate from a few years back that says Woodrow Joseph Livingston."

"We have nothing like that on file."

I freaked out. I could not believe it. Jennifer really had heard my correct name two years before she met me. I realized it was the Lord.

I surrendered my life to Him in the month of March. It was amazing. I simply asked the Lord to forgive me for my sins in Jesus name. I believed that Jesus died for our sins, and I felt joy inside. I had prayed to God when I was homeless, and now that I had a job and a family, there was evidence to prove there is a God.

The Nightmare Solution

Soon Jennifer got pregnant and we moved into a small, cute apartment. One night I had a nightmare. I was pushing Jennifer out of bed, dreaming that she was falling into a black hole. She had to wake me up

The night our daughter, Kassy, was born, I was told that Jennifer and Kassy had to stay in the hospital that night. I went back to the apartment in Caledonia. I was concerned about my nightmares. I was afraid I would hurt Kassy. I prayed and asked God to be in the center of my dreams, to destroy any bad dreams before I went to sleep.

When I fell asleep that night, I was about to have a bad dream when I had vision. A fireball went right through me. I was in awe. I felt as though the uncleanliness was ripped out of me. It was scary and powerful at first, but then I was filled with joy. Fire purges sin.

That night was the last night I ever had a nightmare. All those horrible nightmares—gone! I was so relieved. I was able to see what God was doing, and I acknowledged Him for it.

I started my new life, got married, and surrendered my life to the Lord. Then came my daughter, Kassy, and my son, Andrew. I didn't have much money and I still wanted a professional job. But now that I was with the Lord, I had to trust Him in the walk. God knows me better than I know myself.

I had no idea what to do. I still had the wood shop my friend was renting. I figured that God didn't want me to do that. It was in my past. And besides, cutting two of my fingers on the table saw was the last straw using the wood shop. I gave it all up and said to the Lord, "I trust you that you have a new direction for me and my family."

In the Bible, in the book of Matthew, I found a passage that reads: "Ask and it will be given to you; seek and you will find; knock and the door will be opened to you." My question to the Lord that I've always asked is, "How long?" The author of faith is God, and I had to walk by faith and not by sight. I figured this was going to be an interesting journey, because now I was walking by faith, not on my own.

I started a new hunt for a job. I made countless phone calls and applied for over two hundred jobs. It was the same insanity with the same results as before: a few interviews, and the same old discrimination.

There was this one computer job I applied for in the city of Rochester. The company called, and I was sure I was going to get it. I was asked to come for a third and then a fourth interview. There was a snowstorm the day I went to the fourth interview, with over a foot of snow. The supervisor was the only one there. I drove thirty miles in blizzard conditions. The interviewer didn't bother asking, "How was the drive?" or saying, "Glad you made it safely." All he said was, "Are you ready for the interview?"

I wasn't happy about his questions. He was extremely paranoid about my being deaf and about the company's liability. "Your resumé is great," he said. "But I can't hire you. I'm too concerned about the company's liability."

"Are you kidding me? I drove through a snowstorm and no employee showed up but you, and you're worried about some liability for your company because I'm deaf?"

I left the building. The snow was heavy, and it was windy. I got in the car. I said to the Lord, "Is this a test? Should I sue him or trust that You'll land me a job?"

I took a good advice from my friend Stan, not to sue the company and to trust God.

Jesus said, "Ask and it will be given to you; seek and you will find; knock and the door will be opened to you."

I got back home safely and told Jennifer what had happened. Same old story, same old rejection, and same old discrimination! She tried to encourage me, but nobody seemed to have an answer. I tried to stay focused on God.

I made a call, and the number was mis-dialed. A woman answered. "I think you have the wrong number. Who are you trying to reach?"

"Anyone who is willing to help me get a job."

"I could be of help," she said. "Meet me at my office in Geneseo."

I did just that

"What do you really want to do?" she asked me.

"I want to do CAD, Computer Aided Design," I said. "Many companies are looking for that right now." I told her I needed to take two classes at Rochester Institute of Technology.

She looked it up. She was figuring the costs and wrote me a check right on the spot.

I was stunned and thanked her. I took the two courses and completed the program. Then I started applying for jobs that had CAD work. I got an interview with Garlock in Palmyra, New York through a temporary agency service. I landed the job there.

On my first day, I started working on AutoCAD and Pro/Engineer. I got up from my desk and did an errand. I was at the door where my boss was having a meeting with his boss. I lipread his boss. He yelled at my boss, "Why the heck did you hire a deaf person?"

I was insulted. I walked away wondering if I was going to get booted for being deaf. I was doing my job and my boss really liked the work I was doing. I got along very well with him. I was confident that I was going to get the job permanently if the person who was temporarily disabled didn't come back.

I completed everything I was told to do. It was a six–month temporary job, but I ended up working there for a year. I gained a lot of CAD experience and loved it.

I had to drive almost fifty miles from Caledonia, New York to Palmyra, New York. I didn't mind the long drive, but that summer, there were a lot of thunderstorms in the mornings. It was difficult driving in the storms. Also, I had night vision loss, so it was pretty difficult to see in the dark mornings. I managed, though. I had an issue during the winter months because there was less daylight, but I was allowed to go into work a little late and leave a little early.

A few people were being laid off in that department in the last few months of my contract. When I was finished, on my last day, I visited my boss's boss. I walked into his office and sat down. "You did a good job," he said. "It was nice meeting you."

"I remember on my first day watching you being upset that Garlock had hired a deaf man."

"How did you know?" he asked.

"I can lipread very well. I was watching you from the hallway."

"I'm sorry. You're seen in a much different light than I thought," he said and then shook my hand. "Good luck on your next job. I'll write a good recommendation letter for you."

I thought, *I'll only need that if the company doesn't discriminate against me. But I'm with God, and He made this job happen. He'll certainly make the next job happen.*

Back to the job hunt. It would have been nice if I had been paid for looking for a job because I spent more time looking for a job than actually working for someone.

I was attending church one Sunday and asking people to pray for me to get another job. After church, a woman approached me. "My husband works at a company in Gates, New York. They're hiring. Apply tomorrow and use his name as a reference."

I immediately went to Gates and applied. I had an interview and landed the job right away. The position was assembly and machining. It was a lot of hard work. The job was second shift and I wondered about finding rides or having to drive, since I don't see too well at night. I had no trouble driving to work during the day but driving back home at midnight was hard. It was easy to drive on a country road, but not when it snowed. I always needed the high-beam lights on when driving, but when it snowed, high beams make the view a lot worse. Often, I would have to park the car on the side of the road and wait for someone to drive by and then follow the tail lights as far as I could.

I was still applying for a job in CAD while I worked the second shift. It gave me more time to search for jobs in the daytime.

I prayed. "God, despite all the effort I'm showing you, it's not working. Can you make something happen?"

Then I had a dream. It wasn't a dream of New York State. It looked like Virginia. There were tall trees and a crossroads. Right away, I thought, *New direction. Somewhere farther.*

I started applying on Monster.com and searching for an out–of–state job. I got a quick interview with Grolier Books in Connecticut. They would pay for all my travel expenses to go to an interview.

On the day I left to drive to Connecticut, I was driving along I-90, and the car was acting funny. I thought it was the transmission.

I stopped at a station off the highway. The drive gear is gone," the mechanic said.

"I have to drive to Connecticut for an interview. There's got to be a way to make this work."

"You have another drive gear for highway use. Use first and second gear, then jump to the D-2 gear. But it could all break apart soon."

"Thanks, but I'm going to take that chance."

I did make it to Connecticut for the interview and headed back to Rochester the next day. As soon as I drove into the driveway at home, the transmission died. I looked up in the sky and said, "It had to be You." I went inside and gave my gorgeous wife and kids a big hug.

The next day, I found out I didn't get the job, but I got another interview with Oreck in Mississippi. I had all the arrangements for the flights and hotel, and it was paid for by the company.

I flew into Biloxi in a thunderstorm. As soon as I got to the airport, I was told to go to the car rental place to pick up the car and drive to Oreck. I would have preferred to have someone pick me up rather than drive all over the place trying to read the signs. I finally got to Oreck. I was late for the interview, but it was the thunderstorm's fault, not mine.

The interviewer showed me around the company. While I was following him, it was a little dark in one area. He turned right and I turned left. I started to sweat. I couldn't find him, so I walked the other way quickly, and fortunately I found him. "Are you okay?" he asked

"Yeah. Must be from running all over the place all day." I didn't want him to notice that I had an eye problem, but I thought he probably had noticed. I was thinking, *I blew it. I won't get the job because I didn't see where he was.*

After the interview was over, I thought I was very qualified for the product design position. That evening, I drove along the beaches. I stopped and looked out at the gorgeous ocean. It was beautiful, but it was so humid. I thought I would die if I had to move there.

When I was looking at the ocean, there was a thunderstorm coming up. It was incredible watching lightning striking the ocean. I love thunderstorms, but the sky was darkening, and I had to get back to the hotel so I didn't end up driving like a blind man.

While I was driving back to the hotel, the storm was approaching rapidly, and lightning was striking everywhere. I needed to get to that hotel. I finally saw the hotel sign just as the rain started to pour down

The Wrong Plane

The next day, I flew from Biloxi to New York City. It was a madhouse when I got there. There were more thunderstorms and many delays at JFK. The storms seemed to be following me.

I went to the gate booth of American Airlines and told the woman there, "I'm deaf. Please let me know when my plane is boarding. I'll be sitting right over there, in the corner."

She promised she would do so.

I looked out the window. There were six small American Airlines planes lined up in a nice row. For a couple of hours, I watched the workers speaking into their microphone, wondering what the heck they were saying. I watched a bunch of crazy people moving around like ants fighting over a bread crumb.

"Has my plane has boarded yet?" I asked the woman next to me.

"I have no idea," she said.

I walked through the ant pile crowd and went up to the ticket counter lady for American Airline.

"Go to third plane immediately," she said.

I rushed down the stairs, going outside toward the six planes lined up. I walked to the third plane. I went inside, and there was one seat in the front that was ready for me. I sat down, relieved.

The stewardess shut the door, did her safety talk, and the plane started moving.

I felt weird about the flight, so I asked the guy next to me, "Is this flight heading to Rochester, New York?"

"No, it's going to Washington."

I yelled out to the stewardess, "Stop! I'm on the wrong plane!"

The plane stopped before turning onto the runway. The stewardess opened the door, and I started walking down the stairs.

The ticket lady showed up. "I'm so sorry! I forgot you were deaf. When you were walking out the gate, I was yelling at you to take plane number six."

She walked me to the stairs of plane number six and said, "Have a good flight!"

When I got back to Rochester, a few days later, I got my rejection letter from Oreck. I put it in my rejection pile. "The rejection pile is getting thick," I said to Jennifer. "How many doors do I have to knock on before one open?"

"I do not understand, either," Jennifer said wrapping her arms around me.

"I must keep knocking," I said. "God promised."

I went to a job fair in Rochester and applied for several jobs. I continued working the second shift.

One night, as I was driving home from work, I hit a deer on a dark country road. The car was totaled, and getting hit with the air bag wasn't pleasant, either. It took a good ten minutes for another car to drive by. The driver stopped and asked me if I needed a ride home. I got into his car, and he asked me where I lived.

"Caledonia," I said.

We chatted all the way there and he was a really nice guy. I was blessed that someone took me home.

I kept asking God, "What am I supposed to do now?"

I went to church the following Sunday. I got up during prayer and I said, "Well, I certainly need prayers. I'm deaf, going blind, ran into a deer, totaled my car, and cannot find a white-collar job. I'm at the end of my rope."

One guy stood up and said, "God has something amazing coming for you. I just know it." Transportation was going to be difficult until I could get another car but I was able to find ways to get back home from work through a friend named Steve.

After coming back home from the Million Man March for Christ in Washington, D.C., I went to sleep and had a vision of a trumpet. I woke up from hearing the beautiful sound of a trumpet and jumped out of bed.

Jennifer was still sleeping.

I was deaf, but I had heard a beautiful trumpet sound. It had to be from Heaven. When I heard that sound, I knew God was going to heal my hearing, but I didn't know how, what, or when.

I started sharing my vision that God was going to heal my hearing with a few churches and hoping they would pray for me. Of course, they thought I was crazy. Some people said nasty and cruel things to me, but I thought they were either jealous or judgmental.

Then I got a phone call from Newport News Shipbuilding in Virginia. They wanted to interview me for a senior design position.

Right away, I said to Jennifer, "This is it!"

I flew to Newport News Airport and stayed in a nice hotel. The weather was gorgeous. I took a cab to Newport News Shipbuilding on Washington Avenue.

When I had the interview, I didn't sense any discrimination at all. They verbally offered me the job, and I took the offer.

When I got back home to Caledonia, I walked into our apartment and yelled to Jennifer, "We're moving to Virginia!"

We were all cheering. My daughter, Kassy, was just two years old, and Andrew was not even one yet. I gave my two-week's notice to the company I was working for, and on my last day at work, I gave all the workers a hug. They were all happy for me. I thanked God for such a blessing for my family and me. It was truly incredible how God had planned this out. Walking by faith was the way.

The neighbors gave us a big barbecue, and I gave away some clothes and furniture to them. I had a month before moving to Virginia. I bought a car and drove with my friend Steve to look for an apartment in Newport News.

Driving on Route 64 was very similar to the dream that God had shown me that encouraged me to look for jobs out of state. It was thrilling to be moving to and exploring Virginia.

In the space of one week, I got all the arrangements made for a new apartment and completed the paperwork for the new job. The apartment was gorgeous. The complex had a nice swimming pool and a tennis court.

I drove back to Caledonia and made plans to go out to visit Jennifer's family for a month in Lawrenceville, Georgia. I would stay for two weeks, then go to Newport News to arrange the new apartment.

On moving day, a semi-truck drove into the parking lot. It was a sight to behold as my friends watched the workers pack all our stuff and load it into the truck. Last of all, they drove my car inside. It was a remarkable moment.

Jennifer and I said goodbye to all our wonderful friends.

I even got a surprise check in the mail. It was money that had been owed to me for ten years prior to that time, and I had thought I would never get it back. We were astonished.

Jennifer's face was glowing. "Wow!" she said, "What a blessing God has given you!"

I was overwhelmed with all the excitement. We bought luggage and new clothes and got ready to move. Our close friends, Wes and Connie who lived in Caledonia drove us to the Buffalo Airport. It was hard saying "goodbye."

We flew to Atlanta and stayed with Jennifer's wonderful family. Then I flew to Newport News on my own.

A friend of mine was worried about me being alone in Virginia. "How are you going to get to work or get groceries?" he asked. "You won't have the car for two weeks."

"I'm on a mission for God, whatever I have to do, it will work out."

CHAPTER EIGHTEEN

MISSION FOR GOD

I flew from Atlanta to Newport News. I gathered all my bags, went outside, and got a cab to the hotel, which was two miles from the airport. I had another week before moving to the apartment. It was raining, and I asked the cab driver if he could take me somewhere to eat after I dropped off the bags. He helped me with the bags and waited in the lobby for me as I signed the papers and dropped the bags in my room.

I loved this hotel and the housekeeper remembered me from my last stay. I went to the lobby to meet the cab driver, Jack, and had him take me to a good steak place.

"If you're hungry, I'll treat you to dinner," I told Jack.

"Yeah, I'm hungry."

After dinner, he asked me if I wanted to go anywhere else.

"No, I've got to get unpacked and get ready for work in the morning." But I asked him if he could to take me to and from work every morning and afternoon all week.

I negotiated a deal with him for the week. Everything was working smoothly. It was a mission for God! God made it happen as I knew it would, even though being totally deaf and visually impaired—fear not!

The next morning, I got ready for work, and when I went outside the hotel there was Jack in his car, reading the newspaper and ready to go. During the week, Jack took me to several places. He showed me all around the area. He even took me to Virginia Beach for a tour.

I kept thinking; *Did God send this guy to help me?* He was so nice, and we got along so well.

At the end of the week, it was moving day. I had a week to get the apartment set up before the family arrived. I had to make the kids' bedroom look like home.

Now I was able to drive to work, thanks to Jack who detailed the directions for how to get there. When you're visually impaired, you'd don't want to get lost. I also spent time with Jack, going out to eat or going for a ride. He took me grocery shopping and other places I needed to go to. The guy was an amazing man!

Hurricane Floyd

At Newport News Shipbuilding, we were told that Hurricane Floyd was on a path toward Virginia. I called up Jennifer through the relay service and said to her, "I'm finally going to be in a hurricane!" I told all my friends that I couldn't wait for the storm.

The storm was predicted to hit in the middle of the night, and I was watching the Boston Red Sox while waiting for the storm to arrive. I stayed up all night, because I wouldn't be able to wake up if the wind was that bad or doing damage to the apartment. The winds were not that bad, but the rain was the real issue. There were floods everywhere. The highway near the apartment was flooded with several feet of water, and some of the apartment buildings were flooded. My section was just fine.

I called up Jack. "Let's take a ride and look at the damage."

"Let me see if I can make it to your place first." He thought I was out of my mind.

He got to my place and we took a tour. I was amazed at the floodwater. Some areas were under five feet of water, especially the town of Franklin. I went back to work the next day, but several people couldn't get to work.

My family arrived after spending a month with the children's grandmother, cousins, and relatives. Now our family was back together and adjusting to a new life.

I had to get a lot of things done at work as well. One was having a physical. When I went for the physical, the doctor encouraged me to get a cochlear implant.

"It's something to think about, but I was told by a doctor a few years ago that it wouldn't work for me."

"Technology has improved," the doctor implored. "You're totally deaf. What do you have to lose?"

I discussed it with Jennifer and decided I was going to do it.

I told my boss, Bill, that I had decided to go for the cochlear implant surgery. My co-workers were intrigued and supportive. They were even curious how I would adjust to new sounds.

After an examination by audiologists, I was qualified for a cochlear implant in my left ear. I became even more optimistic that it was going to work. The audiologist told me that because I had been deaf for so long, it could take four years before I started understanding words.

"I'll beat that," I told her.

I had my surgery date all set up. At work, I encountered a nice young woman named Alison, who was a reporter for the local newspaper, the *Daily Press*. She worked for the lifestyle section of the paper. "A friend of yours mentioned to me that you're getting a cochlear implant. Would you like to get together at your place for an interview?"

I said I would, and we arranged to have the interview in the spring. The surgery was not until July. In the meantime, Jennifer and I were looking for a house.

The Cochlear Implant

The photographer and the reporter, Alison, came by our apartment in late spring and started interviewing us. We shared our story and the history of my deafness. Everything was prepared for July. Alison and the photographer were approved by my surgeon to take pictures from the window above the operating room.

The moving date for the new house was in September. I had a lot going on.

During my first year at the apartment in Newport News, I carpooled with a guy Rodney, who was in a wheelchair. He was a nice guy, always happy and friendly. Going to work, I had a lot of trouble seeing in the early morning during the winter because of the short days and my eye disease. Having Rodney with me solved that problem for a short time.

Because the apartment was in Newport News, finding a ride was manageable most of the time. In July, we found a house that was going to be built in Yorktown. It looked like a pretty simple drive from there to work, just a few miles further.

In July, I got ready for my surgery. Jennifer's mom, Betty, was taking care of Kassy and Andrew. Alison and the photographer met me at Virginia Beach Hospital. Jennifer was with me, and she was nervous about the surgery. As soon as she gave me a kiss, I was wheeled into the operating room. The operating room was freezing, but I got knocked out so fast that it didn't matter. Alison and the photographer were at the window taking pictures.

After four hours, the surgery was complete, and I was wheeled out of the freezer. When I woke up, I felt horrible. I threw up blood in a bowl, and the nurse went, "Uh oh!" At first, the doctor thought it was something serious, but he didn't know that when the assistant put the tube down my throat, it was done improperly and made a cut inside my throat. Immediately, they had used a second one and got it through successfully. I had to wait for four weeks before I could get the cochlear processor turned on. I was optimistic and could hardly wait for the day. Alison was giving updates to the *Daily Press* every week on the coming day of my hearing.

The people from the engineering department at Shipbuilding were great supporters. They were all curious how I would hear on my first day. If it hadn't been for Newport News Shipbuilding, I wouldn't have been able to finance the cochlear implant.

My big day arrived. Alison and the photographer came to our apartment to pick up Jennifer and me. They took us to Virginia Beach to see Debbie, the audiologist. We all went into the audio room. Debbie had to tune the implant's processor for twenty-two different sounds. For each sound, she asked me if it felt comfortable in the low range and high range.

Finally, the implant was ready to be turned on. "Are you ready?" Debbie asked.

"Yes!"

She turned it on. I could hear sounds, but I couldn't understand them. Debbie said, "It takes time for the brain to adjust."

Jennifer tried talking to me. I was sweating, trying to understand what she was saying but I felt lost. There were too many noises to identify. I felt like I was dreaming. I just couldn't understand.

Debbie was telling me to relax, and eventually I'd understand the sounds. It reminded me of a story in the Bible when Jesus healed the blind man and at first he saw wavy trees. He couldn't understand what he was seeing. I'm usually an impatient guy. My attitude was I want to hear now, not tomorrow. But you can't force your brain to do something it's not prepared to do, just as you can't force a baby to walk. A baby walks when it's ready. It's the same way with hearing. You have to learn how to hear.

After we left the audiologist and were in the car, it was so noisy, it sounded like radio static. As we drove along the expressway, Alison turned on the radio to see if I could understand anything. I was able to distinguish a few things, such as the sound of a drum playing.

I was annoyed by high pitched noise and everything seemed to be high pitched. Every time I spoke, I felt weird hearing my own voice. I started talking softly and Jennifer had to remind me to speak up. I didn't like my voice at first. I was not used to it. I was so used to merely feeling my voice when I was deaf.

When we got to the apartment the photographer was taking pictures. "I heard the click from the camera!" I told him.

We sat down in the dining room. I was stressed just from hearing for three hours. When I was sitting at the dining room table, all I heard "Tick, tick, tick, tick."

"Is that the clock?" I asked Jennifer.

It was but nobody else had noticed the clock's ticking until I brought it up. It was because the sound was new to me.

I was annoyed by all the sound pollution. When I turned on the television it made me need an aspirin. Alison and the photographer laughed. They headed home. Alison let me know that she would be dropping by on a weekly basis to see how the progress went.

Alison and the photographer came one last time before we moved out of the apartment. I was on my computer and listening to some music and weird sounds. Alison and the photographer watched me select some sounds from the audio CD while the kids were jumping up and down on the bed. I selected an opera singer. She was so horrible that I started laughing really hard. The photographer took a picture of me laughing and put it in the paper. Alison had the whole story put together and had it ready for the Sunday issue on September 10, 2000.

Hearing New Sounds

Jennifer and I got all packed and moved into our new house in Yorktown on the first day of September. The house was gorgeous, and we were excited about it, but I hated living in a house without a basement. It seemed odd to me.

I had to get used to the sounds from outside. When I walked out the front door, I heard crickets in a tree in the front yard. The crickets sounded so loud; it was as though they were jumping on my head. I never had heard crickets before.

I was sitting on the couch one evening when I heard a weird sound from outside. "What was that noise?" I asked Jennifer.

"It's the frogs from the swamp in back."

I couldn't believe that I was hearing frogs. I was amazed. Soon, I was able to identify other new sounds. I would ask Jennifer to name the sound so I could register it in my memory. It was exciting to learn so many sounds I had never heard even as a child. When I wore my old hearing aid I only heard low pitch sounds.

My ability to understand what I was hearing was improving, but slowly. I read books while listening to audio recordings of them so that I could learn to hear the words and register them in my brain. I spent a lot of time practicing.

My good friend and neighbor, Gooch and his family lived across the street. I was talking to him and his next–door neighbor, Charlie on the front lawn of Gooch's house. I heard a strange noise. "Do you hear a ticking noise or something?" I asked them.

They said they didn't, so I tried to follow the noise. I walked toward the Gooch house and finally realized I was hearing his gas meter. Gooch and Charlie had to get pretty close to it to hear it. They were stunned that I could hear it.

"I need a cochlear implant, too!" Gooch said.

I was awfully stressed from trying to hear and to understand speech. At work, all my friends wanted to see if I could hear them. It put a lot of pressure on me. Some of the people had not wanted to talk to me when I was deaf. They didn't know how to, or were afraid, or perhaps they had other problems with deafness. As my understanding improved, many of them started to talk to me more often. The better my hearing got, the more people approached me. I became good friends with one guy who hadn't spoken with me at all when I was deaf.

My cochlear implant changed the perception of my surroundings. It drove me crazy at work when people at the coffee table kept stirring the sugar in their coffee. I could hear the microwave running; it was like a bee buzzing in my ear. Not only that, everyone in the department had earphones and they listened to music while working on their computers. I could hear high-pitched noise all around me.

It was super noisy. I went to use the men's room and inside I heard awful noises. What were they? Then I realized what was happening. It freaked me out and I left the bathroom quickly. Some of my friends were in the hallway.

"I never thought farting noises would be that bad," I said. "From now on, I'm shutting off my cochlear implant every time I go to the men's room."

Hearing new sounds was creeping me out. Sometimes I had to do errands and walk to other buildings to do paperwork. I was easily scared by the cars because of my weak vision. The cars I heard now seemed so close to me that I thought they were going to hit me. I would be crossing the sidewalk and hear a car and I would run to the sidewalk. I felt as though I was being tricked by sounds.

Bill Livingston

At home, I prayed to God. "You handle all my situations. I will not attempt to be recognized and make things happen myself."

It was Sunday, September 10, the day the news story about my cochlear implant, titled "The Gift of Sound," was published on the front page of the *Daily Press*. Jennifer, Kassy, Andrew, and I were ready to look for a church that morning.

When we walked outside to the car, Gooch called out, "Hey, Woody! I read the article about you this morning!"

I gave Gooch a thumbs-up sign and smiled.

My family was in the car as I drove along a country road, and I beeped the horn passing the cemetery. Kassy asked me, "Daddy, why did you beep the horn by the cemetery?"

I chuckled, "I was waking up the dead!"

We drove on a busy street. When I saw a big picnic and outdoor church service under way. "Let's try this one. It looks nice," I said.

She agreed, and the kids had smiles on their faces, as though they were going to a carnival. We attended the outdoor church service. At the end, a man gave a testimony about how he had made his commitment to Christ. He must have been over ninety.

I walked up to him after he got off the stage and told him it was a lovely testimony.

"You look familiar," he said.

"I'm Woody Livingston."

"Oh, my Lord," he yelled out. "My name is Bill Livingston. *Guidepost Magazine* was looking for you. They thought I was your grandfather."

I was stunned. God had made all this happen. Bill was amazed by how God had paved the way for me to receive my hearing. Bill introduced me to his wife, Sarah. She was eighty-nine years old, and they had been married for seventy years. We soon became good friends and had dinner at their beautiful home.

People started contacting me. *Guidepost Magazine* called me for an interview and we made an appointment to meet for four hours in early December at the Marriott hotel. I also had a phone call from a Norfolk TV station. They had heard about my story in the *Daily Press* newspaper. Their news crew came to our house and started interviewing Jennifer and me in the living room. The news reporter, Ginny, asked us a few questions. I was trying hard to understand her but my hearing was still stressful. People assumed I could hear properly right off the bat.

Ginny wanted the whole family to walk to the playground. A lot of our neighbors were outside watching. I mainly wanted to get this thing over with. Jennifer and I took the kids over to the swing set, and I put Kassy and Andrew on the swings. Ginny started asking me questions about my hearing. It was difficult for me to understand everything she was saying, because when I was pushing the kids on the loudly squeaking swings. I had to lipread Ginny and I was sweating trying to understand her.

We all went back to the house, with the neighbor kids tagging along. "You'll be on the 6 o'clock news tonight," Ginny said. Then her phone rang, and she had to rush away to a murder scene in Norfolk. The news crew abruptly disappeared. Two hours later, she called Jennifer and said, "You'll be on the news just after Breaking News."

"Murder beats miracle, right?" I said to Jennifer.

Vie from *Guideposts* was excited to write my story. She was a very friendly woman. She asked me a lot of questions about my deafness and the impact on it by getting a cochlear implant. I shared my testimony about the Lord and how He led me to Virginia. I shared with Vie that God loves giving you surprises you don't expect. I explained how I had thought I would never hear again, even with all the new technology. Miracles from God happen in many different ways and God can point you in a direction to get where he wants you to be. Believing that requires faith. I didn't understand God's entire plan, but I listened as He instructed me what to do through visions and dreams. I was blessed to hear so much better than before.

Vie and her husband invited Jennifer and me to a nice steak restaurant. After we ordered the meals, I said to Vie and her husband, "When you don't expect something and something amazing happens to you out of the blue, it's a gift from God."

After I said that, the owner of the restaurant came to the four of us and said, "Sorry for the delay. Dinner is on me."

Vie and her husband were surprised. "This is from God," I said.

After we had dinner, we went to the Christmas lighting drive-through display. I was listening to Christmas music for the first time since I was a child. I felt so blessed to hear music again. I could hear details of the musical instruments that I had never heard before.

Speaking of music, at home I tried to catch up with Christmas music. I loved listening to "The Little Drummer Boy" or Andrea Bocelli. I started to love music again. At work, all my co-workers brought in CDs for me to download onto my computer so that I could listen to Christian and soft rock music. I loved '50s to '80s music. I loved listening to Pink Floyd because their music was so creative and had so much meaning.

After three months, I was able to understand a few words on the telephone. I practiced calling Jennifer from work as a way of working on listening. I pressed forward on my speech training.

There were so many sounds I had to learn to recognize. One Sunday, I was watching the New England Patriots on TV and the referee blew the whistle. I didn't recognize the sound. When I picked up the phone there was a dial tone. I couldn't believe you could hear a whistle on TV. It amazed me.

Not only that, but I had never realized that you could hear your own stomach noises when you're hungry. It embarrassed me. All these years, my stomach made noises?" I asked Jennifer. A friend came to the house. His stomach was making a lot of noise, so I asked him if he was hungry. He was shocked that I had heard his stomach noises.

Sometimes it was fun to telephone my friends who knew me when I was deaf. I remember calling one friend who wasn't used to talking to me on the phone. "It's okay, I can hear. You can talk to me now."

He was stalling a little. I heard him laughing to his wife, "It's Woody on the phone saying he can hear me."

"I just heard you talking to your wife. I'm not deaf anymore."

He was stunned. It took him time to adjust to talking to me like a hearing person.

When I was deaf, I didn't realize that I was making loud noises. Sometimes I would jingle coins or keys in my pocket. When I heard it for the first time, I realized it could be very annoying. Once I could hear, potato chip bags drove me crazy. They're so much louder than I had realized. When I was at work, I tried to avoid making all that noise involved with folding a potato chip bag. Before, when I was done eating potato chips, I always loved crushing the bag into a ball and tossing it into the trashcan. I stopped doing that once I could hear.

Giving testimonies at local churches was a wonderful experience. I did that at megachurches and small churches. Usually the pastor wanted to be recognized for the healing. When I walked into the lobby in one megachurch, some elders recognized me from the news and the newspaper. They asked me if I wanted to give a testimony about the miracle of gaining hearing.

After worship, the pastor called me up. People were clapping. I took the microphone from the pastor and shared my testimony about how God led me to Virginia and gave me the miracle of hearing.

When I finished, the pastor grabbed the microphone and asked, "How did our church heal you?"

"Nobody healed me. It was God who healed me."

The people said, "Amen!" The pastor's face was red. He was not happy with me. But I took the stand for God. It was disappointing that some leaders wanted to use me to be recognized. On the other hand, some churches didn't believe in miracles. After giving a testimony at one of those, the pastor said, "Jesus did not heal you supernaturally."

"If that's true then Jesus never came down to save your soul."

Some people can be jealous but blessing other people by showing them what God has done in your life is more important than worrying about those who are jealous or mocking you.

After we bought the new house in Virginia, driving was becoming very difficult. It was hard to find carpools because of the other people's schedules. I went to the eye specialist to see how much vision I had left. I had my peripheral vision checked and the eye doctor said, "You have fifteen degrees left in your vision."

Well, I get to hear but now my eyes are getting much worse, I thought

I knew that this was coming sooner or later. I signed up for a bus service to take me to work and back, but the biggest problem was that I was in a different county and the bus would not cross over the border. It got difficult for Jennifer and me. She would have to wake the kids up at 5:30 a.m. and drive me two miles down the road and drop me off. Then I would wait for the bus. Sometimes the bus would be late or not show up at all, and I would have to wait for daylight to walk back to the house and drive the car. Transportation was a real pain. I was increasingly stressed trying to both hear and to handle the transportation.

The Aircraft Carrier

I had to do some research on the *Nimitz* and *Enterprise* aircraft carriers. Since my eyes were getting worse, I didn't know what to do but keep pressing forward. This was my dream job, and I was extremely happy doing it.

Once I got on a ship with a co-worker. I had to walk through the pathways, stairways, and hatches. The ship was under renovation, and it was pretty dim inside. I put a good crack into the safety helmet I was wearing. Everything was in the way, and I kept crashing into things. I almost knocked a Navy woman off the deck as she was working on some wire ways. I never even saw her. She screamed, and my co-worker helped her up. I didn't even see what had happened. I thought my co-worker had run into her. I was getting very banged up following this guy to the destination, up and down flights of stairs, trying not to lose him.

A few days later, I had to do the same thing on the *Enterprise*. I was in the hangar next to the aircraft elevator which was under construction. It was dark and there were no yellow safety straps around. I was about to fall down the shaft when a sailor grabbed me just before I fell in.

"What are you doing?" he asked.

"I had no idea there was an elevator shaft there."

"You could have fallen to your death!" my co-worker said.

"But I didn't fall. I'm on a mission for God!"

I went back to the electrical engineering department, and everybody was talking. Someone made sure to tell me they were going to take out life insurance on me.

"When you go back on the ship next week," my boss said. "I'm sending two assistants for you, one to go in front of you and one behind you, for your safety."

Sexual Harassment?

As a senior designer at Newport News Shipbuilding, I sometimes had to go from building to building to work out details for my drafting work. Once I stopped in an engineering building to talk to a woman named Eileen. I was standing in the pathway next to her cubicle. A woman who was walking by said, "Excuse me."

I didn't know which direction she was coming from because of my tunnel vision. I stepped backwards, thinking she would walk past in front of me. But I was wrong and I pressed against her as she was walking behind me.

She was upset. Eileen was laughing because she knew I had bad eyesight. "I'll talk to her. I know her," Eileen said.

I left the building and went back to my department. I turned on my computer and was sitting at my desk when my boss came to me. "You're being accused of sexual harassment." He was trying hard not to laugh, and all the guys nearby were laughing.

"Is it sexual harassment for a blind man to bump into a woman?"

"This is why we have life insurance on Woody," one of my co-workers cracked.

"I'll take care of this," Bill said.

I had to go back to the building to meet with Eileen. I walked down the pathway and I saw the woman who had accused me of sexual harassment walking toward me. "Hi, Woody!" she said and gave me a big hug. "I'll see you around."

Should I accuse her of sexually harassing me? I thought.

On the way back to my building, after meeting with Eileen, I stopped at an intersection and waited for the "walk" signal to flash. When it started flashing, I started walking in the crosswalk, but a car I didn't see coming sped by me. I walked right into the car but fortunately wasn't hurt. I managed to laugh it off, thinking, *my co-workers are wasting their life insurance money on me.* But all the bumps and bruises was getting discouraging.

The *Guideposts Magazine* story came out in the May 2001 issue. The title of the article was "Back from Silence." A few people were inspired by the story and came to my home to meet me. One man drove into my driveway while my wife and I were standing outside by the front door. He had a framed picture of me with Kassy that he wanted me to autograph. He was truly amazed by my story. He shook my hand and gave me a hug goodbye. I looked at Jennifer. "He framed my picture? Strange."

I was amazed to see how many people were inspired by the news and the *Guideposts* story. I received letters from England, Canada, and many states in the USA. An 88-year-old woman wrote to me and said she went for the cochlear implant after being inspired by the *Guideposts* story. I thought that was truly amazing for a woman her age.

Someone sent me a story from a North Carolina newspaper. I've copied it below.

How a Story Made a Difference

By Kristie Chipps

Denton, North Carolina

Our eight-year-old son, Zacharia, was deaf. For a year he used different hearing aids and other treatments with little success. Finally, my husband and I decided to try a relatively new procedure, a cochlear implant. He had the surgery, began language therapy, and made steady progress.

Still, I wondered if surgery had been right for our son. Sometimes my doubts got me down, like this past May. Looking for something to lift my spirits, I picked up that month's Guideposts. I was stunned to see Woody Livingston's story about his cochlear implant. Reading about his experience reassured me. We had made the right choice for Zacharia.

I was amazed by how many people were inspired to believe there is a God that makes all things possible. We have to walk by faith, not by sight. Faith is about your walking with God, and not alone. The author of faith is God. God has blessed many doctors with the knowledge to perform medical miracles. I believe God has increased knowledge in mankind to give us cochlear implants.

On Sunday, when Jennifer, the kids, and I went to a church where many people knew my story and greeted my family and me. The pastor asked if I would share a testimony, and I did so. Afterwards, I was walking back to my seat when a woman said, "Please heal me. Touch me."

"I'm not God, but we can all pray for you," I said to her.

When I got my hearing, I had to learn how to hear. I had to trust God, even though I can be impatient. God wanted me to focus on Him, since He had brought me to where I had never thought I would be. Even though I was going blind, it didn't mean I lacked faith. It is God's will for whatever His purposes are. We must live for today and not worry about tomorrow.

My boss called me in for a meeting with a few other assistants. They had a report of all the incidents on the ships and in the building. "Your eyes are not getting any better," they said. "We're concerned for your safety." They offered me the chance to take long–term disability. Back then, in 2001, they didn't have the accessibility technology and equipment they do today.

My mission for God is done I thought.

I went home and asked Jennifer, "Do you want to stay in Virginia or go to upstate New York?" She wanted to move upstate, so I put the house on the market. I sold it in a week, and we departed Virginia.

We left with wonderful memories. I'm so thankful to all my friends, families and relatives who prayed for me. I had my hearing, and many people had been inspired by that miracle and the directions God had given me. It had all started from surrendering my life to the Lord and understanding the trumpet vision.

I realized that it takes faith to be able to hear. God gives you the strength, patience and courage to hear better.

CHAPTER NINETEEN

BACK TO NORTH

I flew Kassy, Andrew, and Jennifer to Atlanta, Georgia and rented a U-Haul truck. I had my friend, Steve, from Rochester fly down to Virginia and meet me at the house. I had the house all cleaned out and the truck ready to go.

Steve arrived, and we prepared to leave. I had to go across the street and say goodbye to my buddy Gooch.

Steve and I drove off, beeping the horn to all the neighbors. We drove back to upstate New York, where I dropped off all the furniture and other stuff at my friend's barn in Caledonia. Then I started house hunting. It took a while, but I knew that if I kept praying, God would open the right door. I looked at several houses and I was getting frustrated. I had a few more days before flying down to Georgia.

I started searching the Henrietta area and saw a ranch house. I didn't care for it initially, but I felt something, like a magnet making a connection. My friend Stan came with me to look at the house. The realtor, Bev, was outside on the driveway and was expecting me.

"I want to put an offer on the house," I told her right away.

"You haven't seen the house yet."

"I know, but I'm going to buy it."

Stan and I looked at the house, and it hadn't been renovated since the 70s. But I knew God was telling me to take this house. I didn't care what anybody said. I put the offer down very fast. You can judge me but I knew what God was saying.

We moved from a beautiful, modern big house to an old–fashioned dump. I'll never forget the day when Jennifer and the kids came to

Rochester. Jennifer first walked into the kitchen, and she yelled, "What the heck? Are you out of your mind?"

"Relax. You'll see some interesting changes."

She was disgusted by the interior of the house.

People think I'm crazy, but they don't know what I'm capable of. I love knocking things down and I saw a big, fun project of destruction ahead. I gutted the whole kitchen, bought a table saw and many tools, and built my own cabinets, and renovated the kitchen. Of course, during that time, my wife had to patiently wash the dishes in the bathroom. I finished the kitchen in two months, and then I started knocking down the living room. I've never forgotten the date when I knocked down the living room—September 11, 2001, a shocking day for everyone.

I spent a lot of my time renovating the house, adding patios, a pavilion, a sun room, roofing, and doing many other renovation projects. My friend Wes helped me at times. He also gave me some advice on construction as did the nice people at Lowes Hardware.

My son Andrew used to get all kinds of tools for me when he was little. He learned all the names of the tools and was a good helper. When he grew older, he helped me wire all the switches and outlets. At times, Andrew was my eyes when it came to measurements or color of the wires. We did drywalls, floorings, insulations, paintings, and many other things. He became very handy.

Because of my eyesight, I had so many injuries from the construction that I felt like Tim Allen's character on the *Home Improvement* TV show. One time I had to go to the doctor because I had a strange bump above my ankle. I thought it was a spider bite, but the spot turned out to be stuffed with pieces of drywall and plywood. The doctor cut open my wound and pulled out at least seven pieces of debris. He was baffled.

Sometimes I can't even see a cut until my wife screams and says, "You're bleeding all over the place!"

I've done a lot of plumbing and electrical work in the house. You don't always have to see to know what you're doing. I put a small flashlight in my mouth at times to help me distinguish between black and white electrical wire. I can also feel the smoothness of a copper wire. There's always something to figure out how to do without assistance.

CHAPTER TWENTY

EXPLORING THE OPTIONS

Despite all the projects I had been doing on the house, I wondered about finding a part-time job to stay busy. I never thought about accessibility or support services for the blind. Then I ran into a woman who worked for the Commission for the Blind. Her name was Jane and she provided me with a lot of encouragement. I was stubborn for a while—that is, until I realized that I was going to need to use a cane and learn braille and give up driving. I wanted to explore what the options were for blind and visually impaired people and to see if I could get a decent job like anyone else. Since I had my hearing in my left ear, I thought I would be less discriminated against.

I took a job training course for blind and visually impaired people that was totally pointless and a waste of time and money. I remember that the instructor's first question. "If you were to become an animal, what would you want to be?"

"Come on! What is this?" I said jumping up from my chair. "Employment for *One Flew over the Cuckoo's Nest?*"

Next, the instructor laid out wooden toy blocks. "We are going to see how we can identify what we feel while blindfolded."

I had to get up, walk out of the classroom, and go into the lobby to take a breather. I called my counsellor from the Commission for the Blind. "This program is a joke."

"I know it's not your level, but just finish it, and we'll get together."

I finished and played dumb for the rest of the training.

After one month, our class got together, and the instructor asked everyone what they thought of the job program. One woman responded, "Oh, I love this program! It was fun!"

"Did you get a job?" I asked.

"No."

"Did you get your resumé finished?"

"No."

"Did you get a job interview?"

"No."

"So how in the world could you love this program, if it did nothing for you? Is it because the instructor was all sweet and cute to you?"

Then I asked the instructor, "Did you ever come to work being blindfolded for the whole day?"

"No."

"Did you ever blindfold yourself taking a bus?"

"No."

"Did you write your resumé while blindfolded?"

"No."

"Did you go for a job interview blindfolded?"

"No."

"Then you don't know anything about blind people other than to make them all comfy in their little shell. All you care about is your pay check." I started to see that I had to be wary of people who will treat you like a dog. They'll walk you like a dog, make you sit like a dog, make you stay home like a dog, and make you whine like a dog. The program was totally pointless, especially for those who had a college degree or a professional career.

I've always loved working with numbers. I used to do bookkeeping and I thought maybe I could get a job as a night auditor since my wife used to work at the hotel and I'm good at socializing. I went for a ten week training course in Buffalo. After two weeks, I met with many owners and managers from various hotels in the Buffalo area. I asked them questions about being deaf and blind and finding employment. I asked them to be honest with me because I didn't want to waste my time.

"You must hear the phone perfectly well," they all said.

"Is it okay if you can hear the phone 95% of the time?"

"No."

I visited several more hotels in Buffalo. I asked every single owner, "Would you hire me, knowing that I'm hearing and visually impaired?"

They all said no. They said I would need to have an assistant with me in case of emergencies, fire, theft, and many unexpected situations.

While I was taking this course, I did my own research and learned that I would never get a job at a hotel. I even asked some hotels in the Rochester area and got the same answer. This training was not for the deaf and blind. Most training is just for the blind or visually impaired, and most blind training courses are for call center jobs or phone–related positions. I wanted to work using my brain and hands.

I was not worried about money; I was concerned about becoming bored. I wanted to make sure I knew the things I could do if I went totally blind. I could build a house when blind, but where would I get the money to do that?

I applied to volunteer for many different part–time jobs. I was stunned that I could not even get a volunteer job. Many of the businesses said they didn't want to risk it because of liability. I could hear, but my blindness was a major issue. I decided I was not going through these messy discrimination experiences again. I would just enjoy my early retirement and do some hobbies.

My eyes were fading, and I wanted to be able to function well. I could deal with blindness as long as I could keep busy. It was time for changes, and some were hard to let go, such as giving up driving.

The Department of Motor Vehicles

I was fifty years old and my eyes were declining rapidly. I decided to surrender my driver's license at the DMV and get approved for a handicapped pass.

I got my application approved and the woman returned my driver's license, saying, "Drive safely."

I laughed as I walked out the door. So now I could drive while blind, even after giving the woman proof of my legal blindness in order to get the handicapped pass! I looked at my wife, "Should I buy a jeep because if I don't see the car in front of me I could drive over them?"

"I don't think so!" she laughed.

CHAPTER TWENTY-ONE

SURROUND SOUNDS

I decided I wanted to hear in both ears and would get a second cochlear implant. My old roommate from Gallaudet, Peter had convinced me that hearing in both ears made a huge difference and I was convinced. The funny thing was, I had convinced Peter to get a cochlear implant after I had my first one and then after he had two implants, he was assuring me it was amazing being able to hear in both ears. I was grateful he talked me into getting a second one.

I worked out the financial details, thanks to the Commission for the Blind for their big support. It was the same routine as the first implant. After eleven years, I was under the drill for implant number two. This time the preparation and surgery went smoothly. I didn't get sick the way I had the first time.

A few weeks after surgery, I had the processors set and turned on. It was incredible, but I had to train the other half of the brain. It took a few months to adjust to the new sounds in the right ear. My right ear had been dead since birth. I was surprised that the cochlear implant worked for that ear.

Eventually, I got comfortable with hearing in both ears. It's truly a gift to hear. It helped a great deal while my eyesight was slowly going dark. Hearing in both ears for the first time ever gave me an understanding of where sounds were coming from, such as which direction a car was coming from. It is so useful when you're almost blind and you're listening to footsteps and trying to figure out which direction they're coming from. Now I can actually follow a noise and locate it. It's exciting for me and makes me feel as though I can see.

I felt even more independent. But I did have to be careful of being too independent.

What I love about having bilateral cochlear implants is the music. Oh, what a difference! It's surround sound, and I love it. It's wonderful to be able to hear both speakers, from left and right. When I'm on the couch, I can hear my son's iPhone on my right side and the refrigerator on my left side. Now, I hear very well in conversations. It can be hard when there's background noise, but having bilateral implants helps a great deal.

My wife has been a great supporter, helping me cope with all the sounds and speech. She'll tell me, "That's not the way you pronounce that word." When I want to say a new word, I have to listen carefully to how it's pronounced. A lot of English words are not pronounced the way they're spelled.

My declining eyesight did not stop me from going on a ten-day cruise trip with my in-laws. We had a great time and listening to all the bands and music on the ship, a dream come true. As for my eyesight, it was difficult to see inside some areas of the ship. The dining room was especially difficult. When I went to pick up my food at the counter and told the chef what I wanted, I explained, "I'm visually impaired. Can you please put the plate on my hand so I know where you're handing it to me?"

The chef didn't believe I was visually impaired. He didn't bother trying to hand the plate to me and I couldn't find it. I had to ask the person standing next to me, "Can you kindly tell me where the chef put my plate?"

The kind woman knew I couldn't see well, she brought the plate over to me.

With so many people on the Royal Caribbean cruise, it was difficult to walk around with five-degree tunnel vision, which was like looking through a pipe or toilet paper roll. One morning, I went to breakfast with Jennifer and we sat at a big round table. A waitress was serving coffee. I didn't see her bringing the coffee, and I almost bumped it out of her hand. "Sorry. I'm visually impaired."

"That's okay," she said.

"You're not visually impaired," the guy next to me chimed in. "You're wearing eyeglasses."

"Sir, you obviously have no idea that being visually impaired doesn't mean you cannot wear eyeglasses. I have tunnel vision." He looked away. Some people can be mean, but you've got to let it go.

CHAPTER TWENTY-TWO

THE CARROLL CENTER FOR THE BLIND

I met Don at a monthly support group at the Association for the Blind and Visually Impaired (ABVI) in Rochester. We became good friends, and he encouraged me several times to go to The Carroll Center for the Blind. He assured me that it was a great place for mobility training and for learning braille, woodwork, and even fencing. It was a place to learn to do things independently as a blind person. My Commission for the Blind counselor, Jane, told me the same thing. She said I was very independent and would need to use a cane to remain independent. I always enjoy new adventures and challenges, so I decided to go.

First, I had to take a two-week training session in December to see if I qualified for the three-month Carroll Center program. The city was snowy and mobility training on sidewalks was a challenge. It was my first time touching a cane. I wasn't very bold with it. My group was a wild angry bunch and I wasn't sure if I wanted to get involved in the program. At the end of two weeks, I packed up and waited in the lobby for a cab to Boston's Logan Airport. When we arrived at American Airlines, the cab driver helped me to the lobby. A man who was an assistant for handicapped people came up to me. He was from Latvia and a really nice guy. He took me to check in and then took me to my gate. He was an absolutely charming guy and I tipped him well.

I met up with Jane and she was wondering if I wanted to take the three-month program. I didn't want to because I would have to leave my family for three months. But my wife and friends encouraged me to go for it and so I did.

I flew back into Logan Airport and then took a cab to The Carroll Center for the Blind in Newton, Massachusetts. I got my room on the first floor of a very nice dorm. I checked into my room and dropped my luggage and box in the room.

The resident assistant walked in and introduced himself. "Hi, Woody. I'm Jeff." Right away, he tried to open my box.

"What are you doing?" I asked him.

"Helping you."

"I'm not a five-year-old. I'll take care of it myself."

I got him out of the room and shut the door. It was my first day, and I was a bit concerned that this was going to be a pity–party for the blind. In that case, I would be packing and heading out the door.

I went to the lobby, where I met a visually impaired person and Louise, who was totally blind. I introduced myself and started having a conversation. About fifteen students arrived, and we got our schedules. Classes were Monday through Friday. Weekends were free time.

All the courses were designed to train blind/visually impaired people to live independently. I had to learn how to read braille, how to use a cane, how to cook and manage a kitchen, how to use accessible electronic products, how to live in the seeing world, and so on. I loved the challenges. It takes a lot of training and practice to be blind and live independently. You had to wear blindfolds from 9am to 5pm, Monday to Friday. It was interesting because I had to rely more on my hearing. I had to listen to who was talking and who was in my surroundings.

It was a challenge for me to be in a blind program that didn't understand much about deafness. Most deaf and blind people went to the Helen Keller National Center. I wanted a challenge in the hearing world because I grew up in a hearing world.

Sometimes after classes I would take a walk to get a cup of coffee at Dunkin' Donuts, which was a mile away in Newton Center. The more you challenge yourself using a cane, the better you'll succeed in your independence. Sometimes I'd go with friends. We'd walk to my favorite place, Johnny's, an Irish restaurant.

During mobility training, there was a lot of walking, which was great. Ed was my mobility trainer. He was an awesome guy and I learned a lot. I had to do a lot of walking blindfolded, which was challenging but fun.

I went with Doug to the Quincy Market. After getting off the subway, we had to walk a few blocks to Market Place.

There were a lot of wonderful people I encountered in Boston who would help you cross the street. Or if they realized you were lost; they would come to you and ask if everything was okay. Once I was walking on my own, looking for a barber shop, and I went to the wrong establishment. A gentleman came up to me and asked me if I needed help. I told him I was looking for a place to get a haircut.

"I know where there's one; about half a mile from here," he said. "I can drive you down there if you want."

This nice guy drove me in his Corvette and took me to the barber. He even walked me inside the building. "If you need a ride back to the Carroll Center, I could wait for you and take you back," the man offered. I was pleased to hear that, but I told him I was fine and thank you very much.

There are many more good people than rude, mean ones. If you don't go out and face the consequences of being blind, you won't know how many good people are out there who would help you. Some people are afraid and won't face the challenge. Some blind or visually impaired people make excuses for why they can't go grocery shopping or visit a friend. The Carroll Center is a place where they teach the blind and visually impaired to be independent. It's important to be trained. I would not want to rely on my wife all the time to be my cane.

My group and I decided to go to a Red Sox game. The staff at Fenway Park met us at the gate at 5 o'clock. It was an interesting evening and we all walked through the crowds on the sidewalk, trying to stay close to each other. Louise and Joe are totally blind, while Doug and

John are visually impaired like me. Unlike me, though, they can hear very well. When we met the assistant at the gate at Fenway, he used his voice so that we could follow him. I can't tell the direction a sound is coming from as well as a hearing person can, but we were all acting as a team and trying not to lose each other. It was challenging, especially in the dark areas at Fenway.

When we got to our seats behind the plate under the roof, we were given radios that were commercial free. They were really convenient for visually impaired and blind people. I was impressed by the narration on the radio. All the details of the game were very clearly described.

The game was delayed by an hour and a half due to a big thunderstorm. I challenged myself to get up and get drinks for us. There were many people walking in the pathway, which was pretty dark. While I was walking through the crowd with my cane, a guy pushed me down and said, "You're not blind."

A woman pushed him away and helped me up. "Where do you need to go?" she asked.

"To the concession stand and thank you."

She walked me to the stand, and I ordered hotdogs and drinks. I asked the woman if she wanted anything, but she politely declined. I told her that I could manage to get back to my seat. She smiled and went away. Then I realized that I had made a mistake. I had to carry three drinks, three hotdogs, and my cane. Ed, my mobility trainer, always said, "No multitasking." And here I was, trying to do just that.

"I'm not sure I can handle this," I told the vendor.

He asked for a volunteer to help me. A nice woman took the drinks and hotdogs and followed me as I found my way back to my seat. I gave my friends the drinks and hotdogs and thanked the woman.

There are probably more nice people than there are mean ones. You just have to let them know you need help and not assume that nobody cares. During the game, the guy behind us generously bought all of us hotdogs because Doug was calling out for an assistant for hotdogs and couldn't get the assistant attention.

I had another challenge to walk and find the men's room. I had to look for the stairs and go down one level. To me, the stairway was very dark. I was going down the stairs too impatiently and walked into a wall. A woman saw me and asked if I needed help. "Yes," I said, and she led me to the doorway of the men's room.

I went in and had to figure out where the urinals were. Then I had trouble finding the sink. A young kid helped me find it. What a blessing that kid was! I was amazed. I hadn't thought a young kid would help a visually impaired person.

Finally, I left the bathroom and tried to find the long, dark path to my seat. I started walking along the pathway, and another guy poked me on my shoulder and said, "You're not blind!"

I was stunned. Two in one night! A woman overheard him, came to me, and asked if I needed help. I told her I needed to find the stairs. I said I should be able to find my way from there. It seemed to me that when you know the complete layout of Fenway Park, finding your way around inside it should be as simple as walking in your own home.

Using the cane gave me the boldness to do more things independently, like getting up in a restaurant and using the restroom. When you're using a cane, people know you need help, and sometimes they offer to help you.

It took time to not let it bother me when people stared at me when I used a cane. Once some kids asked me what "that stick" was, and I told them, "It's a spy stick."

They asked their mother, "can you buy me one?"

Their mother laughed.

At the Carroll Center, I enjoyed taking fencing. The purpose of fencing was to teach the blind and visually impaired to control their balance and stance. When I walked on the sidewalk, I had to be able to maintain my balance and walk straight.

One morning, I walked into the building and Ralph Macchio was standing in the lobby, which we called the Fish Bowl.

"Hey, you're the Karate Kid, right?" I asked.

He smiled. "That's right."

The desk clerk said to Ralph, "That's Woody."

Ralph shook my hand, and the desk clerk took our picture.

Going out to places on weekends was a lot of fun. I would go to Quincy Market and on a tour of George's Island. It's a beautiful scene of Boston Harbor looking at the skyscrapers of Boston.

After I spent the day at Quincy Market with two friends from the Carroll Center, we had to take the dark subway back to Newton. The guys went ahead of me in the crowd. I was listening to the speaker announcing what train was about to come. I had no idea if this was the Green Line, and I couldn't find where the other guys were. People rushed into a train, so I decided to go into that train. It was crowded, and a man offered me a seat. I sat down and chatted with people. I was having a nice conversation with five people. Then I asked, "Does this train stop at Newton Center?"

"No, you're on the wrong train, but I can get you on the right one."

This nice gentleman and I got off the train together. He took me through the dark in the crowd and we waited for the right train. When my train arrived, he put me on it and shook my hand.

Now that I was on the train to Newton Center, I asked a few people if they were going to Newton Center, so I would know it was my stop when they stood up. The train stopped at Newton Center, and a woman tapped my shoulder and said, "This is the stop."

I walked out of the train to the platform. I knew the routine because Ed, the mobility trainer, had shown me a few times how to find the way with my cane. While I was walking, the two guys from the Carroll Center I had gone with, Doug and John, were just getting off the train. I sneaked up to them and scared them.

"Where were you? We thought you got lost!"

"Aren't I trained to do this on my own?" I said with a laugh.

During a meeting for all the students from the Carroll Center, this train trip was brought up. I explained to the students, "There's no need to panic. You're not going to end up in California if you get on the wrong train. Sometimes getting lost can be beneficial. It was fun for me. I met some interesting people. Being blind or visually impaired, you have to learn to do things independently, that when a situation arises, you'll be able to handle it on your own."

I spent some weekends with my cousin Danny, going on boat tours and fishing off Salisbury Beach. At one point, we ran into dolphins. There were countless numbers of them; they were everywhere.

Another weekend, my friend Bob from Connecticut picked me up and took me to his beach house in Waterford, Connecticut. For me, the challenge is to confront all new things and not worry about what I can't see. Bob and Judy showed me their beach house and mapped out where everything was so that I could do things myself. I had a great time going on boat rides to Mystic Beach and along the coastline. It was an adventure and they were such a blessing.

Another time, my friend Mike took me to Long Island for our friend Scott's fiftieth birthday celebration. I met up with all my Long Island buddies. It was difficult for me at the reception because the band was loud and the place was too dark for me. The biggest mistake I made was not having brought my cane with me. I was lost, but many kind people helped me around. A cane would have made things easier.

I also took a few trips to New Hampshire during my stay in Newton to see Billy and his family. There were a lot of wonderful times at the beach and having family cookouts. I was glad I could hear everyone, even though I couldn't see them well.

My friends and my cousin Danny made my three–month stay at the Carroll Center an adventure. Seven of us graduated from the center. A lot of people hated to leave there because we were like family. However, we had to go back to our hometowns and face the obstacles of being blind or visually impaired.

I walked into my last fencing class early as I sat down to open a letter I got in the mail. It was from my sixteen-year-old daughter Kassy, I opened the letter and started reading it,

"Dear Daddy, how are you? How's it going at the Carroll Center? Are you really going blind? Are you going to be able to see me when you get back home? I'm scared...I hope you don't go blind. I can't wait to see you when you get home...I love you daddy!"

Tears were rolling down my cheeks and I couldn't read the letter any further. It hit me so hard, I couldn't believe how much my daughter cared. It was something that made me realized how much my family really loves me as much as I love them.

At the end of my speech at the graduation, I said, "May the cane be with you!" I was finally bold in using mine.

Once again, I arrived at Logan Airport. When I entered the American Airways section, an assistant approached me and gave me a hug, he was the same guy I met the last time I was there. Then he walked me to the concession stand, where the vendor said, "It's on the house." I had a cup of coffee and a snack. The assistant helped me to my gate and seat. He also showed me where the men's room was. He was extremely helpful; a wonderful guy. Thanks to Logan Airport for hiring this man. Handicapped people need people with good hearts.

I was excited to be back home with my family. I got a fire going in my backyard in my fire pit and sat with my good old neighbor I'd known for years. We sat the patio by the fire.

Since it was dark, I asked him, "Where are you?"

"I'm over here."

"Where is here?

"Right here"

"Are you in front of me or right or left side of me?"

"I'm right in front of you, don't you see me?"

No matter how many times I explain to some people that I see like looking through a straw, they still don't get it. I have to use my toilet paper roll demonstration so they'll understand what it's like to have tunnel vision.

There are many wonderful people willing to help. A few unkind, inconsiderate people would never be able to stop me from achieving things. When I faced any obstacle in my life, it helped me learn about myself and about people. I have always believed in pushing forward and working hard—taking any opportunity to make my life better. The Lord gives me strength and courage to walk by faith, not by sight.

ABOUT THE AUTHOR

Woody Livingston and his wife, Jennifer, have been married since December of 1995. They have two children, Kassandra and Andrew. Woody continues looking for new adventures and challenges every day. He is involved with the deaf/blind community and gives inspirational testimonies to various groups and organizations. He holds a B.A. degree in industrial design and retired from Newport News Shipbuilding as a Senior Designer. He enjoys woodworking and many outdoor activities. He also loves to travel and listen to music.

Made in the USA
Lexington, KY
12 July 2019